Journey to The Top 3% League

Unlocking The Hierarchy of Human Excellence

Rajeev Kharyal

Made with ♥ on the Notion Press Platform
www.notionpress.com

Victory is in the mind;
if you win in your mind, you win.
Defeat is in the mind;
if you give up in your mind, you lose.

Shree Swami Satyanand Ji Maharaj

Table of Contents

Page No

Introduction

From survival to Purpose

Throughout human history, our existence has been about more than just survival. Early humans, despite living without written language, complex tools, or a deep understanding of the world, discovered fire—a turning point that sparked creativity, connection, and purpose. This marked a shift from mere survival to building societies.

As humans evolved, we began to dream, create, and form meaningful connections, propelling us toward a deeper sense of purpose. With societal advancements, our lives became more complex, and we sought relationships, achievements, and fulfillment

The Challenge of Today

In today's digital age, constant noise and distractions threaten to affect us. The challenge now is to cut through the noise and uncover what truly matters.

The Journey Begins

This is where our modern journey begins—to live intentionally, with connection and purpose. Discovering Your Path to Fulfillment requires understanding yourself and the world around you.

Understanding Yourself and Others

Over years of observation, I've noticed that people approach life's challenges and opportunities in different ways. These differences can be grouped into three broad categories. This framework isn't meant to limit anyone—it's meant to help you reflect on where you are and inspire you to move forward.

The Three Categories

1. Bronze (IQ) – 84%:

The "doers" of the world, primarily driven by logic, problem-solving, and hard work, yet often limited by a lack of emotional awareness. Focused on external achievements, they seek material validation and work tirelessly to make a living. However, they often experience an ongoing sense of dissatisfaction, feeling as if something essential is missing. It is like donkey tireless carrying a heavy load, they may rarely pause to enjoy life or explore beyond daily tasks.

2. Silver (EQ) – 13%:

The "thinkers." They blend intelligence with emotional awareness, striving to understand both themselves and others. Committed to personal growth, they often seek success and enjoy life's pleasures. However, their focus is largely centered on themselves—on building a good life for their own happiness. Like a well-trained horse, they move steadily along their path but may stop short of finding a purpose that extends beyond their personal needs.

3. Gold (SQ) – The 3%:

The "holistic achievers." They possess not only high IQ (intelligence) and EQ (emotional intelligence) but also a high Social Quotient (SQ). This combination enables them to live with purpose, uplifting others as they grow themselves. They find true fulfillment by contributing to the greater good.Like bees tirelessly supporting their hive, they live guided by values, flexibility, and a sense of shared responsibility. Even in the face of challenges, they remain focused on their mission to make a positive impact.

Your Journey to Fulfillment

Take a moment to reflect: Which group resonates with you the most? This book is your guide to moving forward—whether you're a Doer, Thinker, or Holistic Achiever. It offers tools and insights to help you rediscover purpose, build deeper connections, and create a life filled with lasting fulfillment.

The Power of Intent

In today's fast-paced world, it's easy to focus on what we do without thinking about why we do it. Intent is more than just a motivational buzzword—it's the compass that aligns your actions with your values and long-term goals. Intent helps you break free from distractions, stay connected to your purpose, and unlock your true potential.

A Personal Story

For years, I believed success was all about intelligence—achievements, titles, and accomplishments. But over time, I realized that without emotional and social intelligence, traditional success feels empty. Fulfillment doesn't come from accomplishments alone. It comes from aligning your actions with intent and living a life of purpose rather than simply going through the motions.

A Moment of Clarity

When I was young, I had a moment that changed how I saw life. During a visit to the Delhi Zoo, I noticed something that stayed with me. The animals were kept in enclosures designed to mimic their natural habitats. They had food, shelter, and safety, but something was missing—freedom. These animals, though alive, lacked the vitality and purpose they might have had in the wild.

A Parallel with Human Life

I saw a parallel with how many people live. Especially in structured environments like corporate settings, we can feel confined. These systems may provide stability and security, but they can also limit self-expression and personal growth. Unlike the animals in the zoo, we have the power to change our circumstances. We can break free from invisible barriers and pursue a life that goes beyond societal expectations.

The Journey Ahead

The journey from 84% or 13% to the Top 3% requires courage, reflection, and a willingness to challenge the status quo. Surprisingly the energy required to reach to the Top 3% is often less than the effort many expend to remain in 13% Or 84%- the journey is not about working harder ; it's about understanding and embracing a few essential principles. The rewards are worth it: a life of meaning, freedom, and fulfillment.

From insights to Action

In a world where generic formulas fall short, this book introduces a groundbreaking framework for achieving fulfillment. We'll simplify complex concepts from management schools across various subjects, topics on psychology and other domain experts into actionable insights, using relatable analogies for common people. Successful individuals from diverse fields share a common viewpoint: adopting personalized strategies and practical interpretations tailored to their unique needs. Apply this adaptable framework to unlock your own unique journey, tailored to suit you.

The 3A Framework: Your Path to Fulfillment

To guide you on this journey, I introduce the 3A framework:

1. Awareness: Recognize where you are and what needs to change. Take an honest look at your life, acknowledging your strengths, weaknesses, and areas for growth.

2. Acceptance: Embrace your reality as a starting point for growth. Acknowledge that your current situation is not a reflection of your worth, but rather an opportunity to learn.

3. Action: Take small, purposeful steps toward a more fulfilling life. Set SMART goals (Specific, Measurable, Achievable, Relevant, Time-bound) that align with your values and intentions. Celebrate your progress, learn from setbacks, and continue moving forward.

By applying the 3A framework, you'll be empowered to transform your life, unlocking your full potential and living a life of purpose, connection, and fulfillment.

Chapter 1

The Big Fat Divide

Understanding the Divide
that you can not always see

In today's world, conversations often focus on the divisions that exist in society. These divides manifest in many ways—differences in wealth, opportunities, access to resources, social status, and even identity conflicts. These divisions aren't new; they've existed for as long as society itself. Whether in our jobs, personal lives, or communities, we all encounter these divides at some point.

But here's a question: Is this divide an unchangeable part of life, or is it something we've accepted without questioning?

Many of us feel weighed down by these divisions, but some have learned to recognize the forces that shape this system and navigate them in ways others don't. This divide is not always easy to recognize. It's woven into the fabric of our daily lives, often hidden behind the routines and beliefs we've been taught to accept. Society conditions us to believe that the struggles we face are just "the way things are," making it difficult to imagine what lies beyond the walls that confine us.

Think of it like walking through a dense fog. You sense that there's something more out there, but the fog—representing your belief system—keeps your vision limited. It tells you that where you are is as far as you can go. But what if you pushed through that fog? What if there's a whole new world of possibilities on the other side?

There's a story that illustrates this idea perfectly, known as

The Frog in the Well.

In this simple tale, a frog lives its entire life in a well, believing that the well is the entire world. One day,

a turtle visits and tries to explain that there's a much larger world beyond the well—one with vast oceans, forests, and skies. The frog, however, refuses to believe this. To the frog, the well is all there is. It might seem like a simple children's story, but it holds a profound lesson for all of us. *How often do we, like the frog, remain stuck within our own limited perspectives, unaware of the possibilities that exist beyond our immediate surroundings?* Our beliefs, shaped by society and our experiences, confine us. And it's these unseen limitations—the hidden divide—that keep us from reaching our full potential.

As Aristotle wisely said:

> **66**
>
> *It is the mark of an educated mind to be able to entertain a thought without accepting it.*
>
> **99**

Before we can break free, we need to recognize that there's more beyond the walls of our current understanding.

The Routine Trap: Working but Not Moving Forward

The first step in overcoming this divide is recognizing that it exists. That's what this book is here to help you do—not to reinforce the division, but to shine a light on it so you can see it clearly. Once you understand it, you can start taking steps to break free. The goal here isn't just awareness—it's empowerment. By learning about the forces that create this divide, you'll be better equipped to navigate it and find a life of greater fulfillment.

Mahatma Gandhi put it best:

> **66**
>
> *You must be the change you wish to see in the world.*
>
> **99**

Sometimes, moments in life can reveal deeper truths about the divide we face. I remember an experience early in my career that opened my eyes to this reality. I was sitting in a cubicle, overhearing a conversation between two of my colleagues. One of them was carrying a stack of files and made a remark that has stayed with me ever since:

"My headaches are just like our expense reports—both are never-ending," she said.

The other replied, "I sort of get it. What do you mean exactly?"

"Well," she explained, "every month, more and more data gets dumped on our desks. We try to make sense of it, and just when we think we've got it figured out, more comes in. It feels like no matter what we do, it never ends."

Her words struck me deeply. At the time, it seemed like a typical work complaint, but the more I thought about it, the more it reflected a common feeling many of us share: the sense of working tirelessly without ever seeing the bigger picture. This is a consequence of the divide—feeling stuck in systems that don't seem to reward us or lead to meaningful progress.

Most of us live in a routine that can feel like a never-ending cycle. You wake up, go to work, come home, and do it all again the next day. The work piles up, and no matter how much you accomplish, it feels like you're not moving forward. It's not just about the work itself—it's the feeling of being trapped in a grind that never really ends.

We spend the week looking forward to the weekend, but when it finally arrives, we're too exhausted to enjoy it. And before you know it, Monday is on the horizon again. ***It's like living in a system that keeps you moving forward just enough to keep going, but never enough to break free.***

As Robert Brault once said:

> **"**
> *We are kept from our goal not by obstacles*
> *but by a clear path to a lesser goal.*
> **"**

Think about how we treat the weekend—as if it's borrowed time. *We work all week, hoping for a chance to breathe, but when the weekend comes, it often feels too short to really recharge. And then, before we've even recovered, we're back in the grind, feeling just as tired as before.* This carrot-and-stick system keeps us moving, but moving toward what? Promotions, paychecks, and recognition can provide short-term satisfaction which do happen, but they don't always lead to true fulfillment.

Conditioning and Comfort: How Our Beliefs Hold Us Back

This brings us to another story that illustrates the hidden divide: **The Elephant Tied to the Rope.** When an elephant is young, it's tied to a rope that's strong enough to keep it in place. As the elephant grows and becomes more powerful, it could easily break free from the rope, but it doesn't even try. Why? Because it's been conditioned to believe that the rope is stronger than it actually is. Even though it has the strength to break free, the elephant remains mentally trapped.

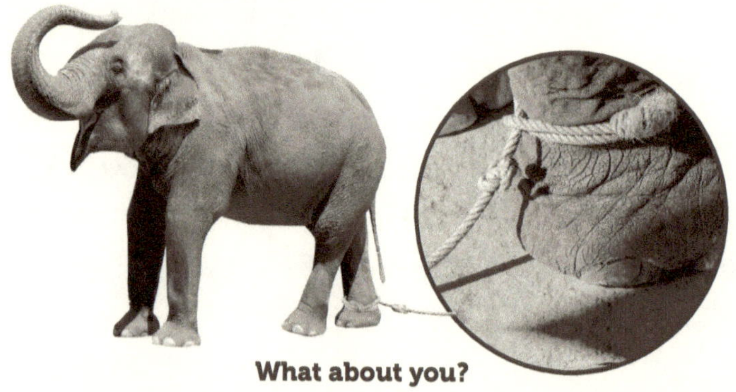

Many of us are like that elephant—held back not by physical limitations, but by the beliefs we've internalized. We believe that we can't break free from the systems we live in, even though we have the power to do so.

For many, the comfort of staying on a well-paved path is enough. There's security in following societal expectations: going to school, getting a stable job, starting a family, and eventually retiring. These paths offer acceptance and stability, but they often limit our potential and imagination. For those who desire for something more, breaking free from this divide requires overcoming internal barriers—the doubts, fears, and beliefs that hold us back.

It's important to remember that this divide affects everyone, even those who appear successful. Think about celebrities endorsing products that don't align with healthy or authentic lifestyles. Despite their fame and wealth, they too are trapped in systems driven by external expectations—systems that value profit over authenticity.

It's a paradox. Even people who seem to have it all can feel stuck. Research shows that humans are wired to follow high-status individuals. We mimic the behaviors of those we admire, which explains why celebrity endorsements work, even when the products aren't in our best interest. But just like us, these celebrities are caught in their own version of the divide.

Breaking Free: Shifting Mindset Beyond Wealth and Status

Ultimately, this divide isn't about how much money you have or what your status is. It's about mindset. The good news is that once you recognize the divide, you can begin to break free. And that's what this book is here to help you do—empower you to push through the fog, escape the well, and break the rope that's been holding you back.

Chapter 2

The Social Engineering

> **The quality of life we experience is very telling of our position in the societal divide**
>
> – Rajeev Kharyal

Introduction to Social Engineering

Society often operates through an invisible set of rules and structures that shape our actions and thoughts. These rules, though unwritten, define what is acceptable, desirable, and even possible for individuals. Whether we recognize it or not, we are influenced by social pressures, often conforming to standards set by external forces.

In this chapter, we will explore how societal norms, illusions of freedom, and personal limitations affect our behavior and decisions, often without our conscious awareness. *From historical examples to philosophical insights, we will uncover the subtle mechanics of social engineering and how it maintain a hidden hierarchy.*

The Emperor's New Clothes and The Illusion of Freedom

One popular folktale that resonates deeply with the theme of societal pressure is *The Emperor's New Clothes* by Hans Christian Andersen. It's the tale of an emperor who admired his appearance and status above all else. Obsessed with his image of power and prestige, he becomes an easy target for two cunning weavers.

These weavers boast of their exceptional skills and pose as manipulative con artists, preying on the emperor's insecurities and ego. They deceive him by claiming that their fabric has magical properties, making it invisible to anyone who is incompetent or unworthy of their role. Fearing the embarrassment of being deemed unworthy or ignorant, the emperor and his courtiers pretend to see and admire the non existent clothes.

As the emperor parades through the town, driven by the fear of social judgment, the townspeople too conform to the illusion. No one dares to question the farce, unwilling to risk appearing foolish or out of place. The pressure to conform becomes overwhelming—until a courageous child, untainted by the fear of judgment, speaks the truth, revealing the emperor's nakedness to all.

Andersen's story masterfully illustrates the powerful influence of societal pressure on individual behavior. This pressure compels individuals to act in ways they otherwise wouldn't, often against their own better judgment. In modern times, we can see this dynamic play out in consumer culture and social norms. *Products, trends, and even lifestyles are marketed in a way that makes them appear essential for fitting into society. Social expectations and the desire for acceptance drive individuals to conform, even when their choices may not align with their true preferences or values.*

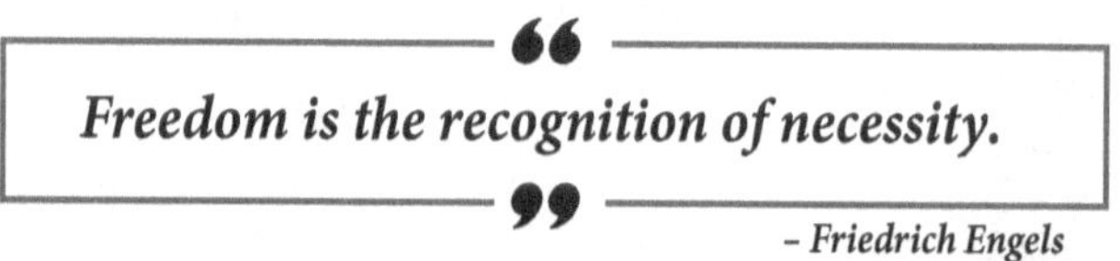

Friedrich Engels once said that true freedom comes from understanding the limits we face, and this idea invites us to think differently about the very concept of freedom.

Taking this a step further, the French philosopher Michel Foucault argued that what we often perceive as freedom is, in fact, a carefully crafted illusion. Sure, it feels like we have the power to choose, but our decisions are frequently shaped by invisible forces—societal norms, power structures, and the expectations placed upon us. Foucault believed that freedom isn't just something we automatically have; it's something we need to actively work toward, requiring conscious effort and awareness of the forces that guide us.

Consider the world around us today. We often believe that we are freely choosing our careers, lifestyles, and even our opinions. But if we take a closer look, we can see the subtle ways that external pressures influence these "choices." Whether it's the media shaping our worldview, cultural standards defining success, or economic pressures narrowing our options, our sense of autonomy is often manipulated without us even realizing it.

But there's hope. The first step toward reclaiming our freedom is recognizing this illusion for what it is. *By understanding how societal conditioning shapes us, we can begin to break free from the constraints and start living more authentically. True freedom, then, is not just the ability to choose—it's the ability to choose with awareness, fully conscious of the pressures we face and actively deciding to move beyond them.*

The Daily Grind and The River of Limitations

Our living cultures are constructed in ways that exhaust us and leave us with no energy. We expend our time and energy on unfulfilling jobs and spend the leisure time replenishing that energy through alcohol or any other substance, merely to go back to our jobs the next day. We internalize that as a reward, so we are fooled by the dopamine released in our brain to keep us stuck in this toxic cycle.

However, there is another form of manipulation that doesn't involve substance abuse but people. There are individuals who manipulate and exploit others, using their influence to control and shape opinions on a larger scale. Since the power of manipulation can sway the beliefs of individuals or groups, by doing so one achieves selfish objectives with ease.

When one doesn't conform to societal beliefs, one carries the risk of

rejection and criticism. Fear of being judged, failing, or being left out makes people hesitant to do anything different. This fear keeps things the same and makes people feel like they have to stick to what's 'normal,' even if it's not really what they want or what will make them happy in the long run.

This notion of being stuck in a loop—whether by societal norms, fear, or addiction—is reminiscent of a story I once heard, which illustrates the subtle but powerful ways we can be trapped by our own actions or inactions.

Many years ago, when the road to Rishikesh was treacherous, and travelers preferred to journey by boat along the serene river flowing from Haridwar, four friends decided to embark on such an adventure. They set off at midnight, filled with excitement, estimating that their four-hour ride would bring them to Rishikesh by dawn.

As they pushed off from the Haridwar shore, the friends felt exhilarated, their laughter and chatter mingling with the gentle lapping of the water against the boat. The night wore on, and the friends continued to row, their spirits high, as the sound of the waves created a soothing melody.

Finally, after what seemed like an eternity, the first light of dawn crept over the horizon. The friends looked around, expecting to see the familiar sights of Rishikesh. Instead, they found themselves at a shore that seemed eerily familiar.

Confused, they approached a sadhu sitting by the river and asked, 'Is this Rishikesh?' The sadhu barely acknowledged their presence, and the friends thought he hadn't heard them.

Undeterred, they approached another sadhu, who seemed more willing to engage. 'Have we reached Rishikesh?' they asked again. The sadhu looked at them with a piercing gaze and replied, 'You still have to go if your destination is Rishikesh.'

The friends were perplexed. 'But we've been rowing all night!' they exclaimed. The sadhu looked around the boat and smiled calmly and said, 'You never untied the boat from the mooring rope.'

The friends' hearts sank as they realized their mistake. They had been rowing in circles, never actually leaving the Haridwar shore. The sound of the waves had lulled them into a false sense of progress.

As they stood there, feeling foolish and defeated, the sadhu's words struck a chord. They realized that they had been like the boat, stuck in one place, never making progress toward their goals. They had been passing time, but not growing.

This story serves as a metaphor for the lives of many individuals who are part of the 84 segment. Just like the friends who thought they were making progress, many people in this segment believe they are moving forward in life, only to realize that they've been stuck in the same place all along. The daily grind, much like the waves against the boat, creates an illusion of progress. We mistake motion for growth, failing to see that we haven't untied ourselves from the moorings that keep us in place.

The sadhu's message is clear: real progress requires awareness and intentional action. It requires us to untie the ropes of complacency, fear, and societal expectations that bind us. Only then can we truly set off on a journey towards growth, self-discovery, and fulfillment.

Groupthink: The Power of Collective Illusion

"When you're part of a group like that, you start to think like the group, not yourself."

A powerful example of groupthink and collective illusion can be found in the marketing campaign for "Lucky Strike" cigarette brand in the 1920s. To tap into the growing female demographic, Lucky Strike associated smoking with freedom, slimness, and modern femininity. Public relations pioneer Edward Bernays was hired to craft a campaign that positioned smoking as both a fashionable and empowering choice for women.

One key element of the campaign was the placement of dieting manuals inside Lucky Strike cigarette packages, subtly promoting the idea that smoking could curb appetite and help women maintain a slender figure. The iconic slogan, "Reach for a Lucky instead of a Sweet," reinforced this idea by framing cigarettes as a healthier alternative to indulgent sweets, linking smoking with self-control and beauty. Advertisements featured glamorous, sophisticated women, embedding the notion that smoking was a symbol of elegance and liberation.

This marketing strategy was highly successful, boosting Lucky Strike's market share by over 200%. However, while the campaign resonated with societal ideals of appearance and freedom, it also exemplified the power of collective illusion. Women who adopted smoking, believing it to be an expression of independence and sophistication, were ultimately manipulated into prioritizing external appearance over internal well-being. The dangers of smoking were masked by a seductive narrative of empowerment, showing how groupthink can foster deception and manipulate behavior on a mass scale.

The Hidden Hierarchy and Impaired Vision Towards Excellence

All of it is not merely a result of chance or personal preference. No, there's a hidden hierarchy at play—a societal code most of us haven't even begun to decipher.

The code that controls society has been ingrained not only in our psychology but also in our stories. It is through these lores that I came across what would become the grounds for my framework.Our elders have recounted different versions of the stories of 3 and 13 for many years [Teen (3) aur Terah (13)].

The phrase

> **66**
> *Na toh tum teen mei ho na hee terah mei*
> *(you are neither in the threes nor in the thirteens)*
> **99**

was often used to convey that our actions do not produce any value, and therefore, we cannot be considered a part of the 3 or 13.

These stories guide us in the direction of making meaningful decisions. They are like warnings. It reminds us that our choices determine our place within this societal framework. To be among the '3' or the '13' is not about numerical superiority but about clarity of vision. It's about being able to read the room. It's about knowing your position in society and the quality of your contributions to the world.

As an adult, I reflected on these stories and compared them with my own observations. I notice that people who possess the qualities of segments 3 and 13 tend to act in ways that add value to the world. Their actions are motivated by a desire to achieve excellence, which drives them to have a positive impact. However, I have also observed that our elders often disregard those who do not possess these two characteristics, which has led me to perceive that the other

84 out of 100 (keeping 100 as a standard for understanding) individuals who lack introspection hence engage in activities that do not contribute to their personal growth and development. They follow a routine trapped in mundane pursuits where meaningful takes back seat. Their vision is clouded by various external factors and internal challenges that prevent them from seeing a clear picture of the world.

The '3' and '13' groups of people are driven by a deep desire for excellence and impact. They see through the fog that blocks the path of the majority, giving them a clearer sight. This clarity then guides their actions towards a sense of purpose and responsibility. It also pushes them to seek meaningful aspirations.

Impaired vision, both literal and metaphorical, can be compared to an actual loss of sight. When a person's eyesight deteriorates, everything becomes blurry, prompting a visit to the doctor. One of the most common tests at the ophthalmologist's office is the *visual acuity test, where you read letters from an eye chart. As the letters get smaller, they become harder to read, and the doctor assesses your vision's sharpness based on how well you can identify them.*

The eye chart is typically placed 6 meters away, with the bottom row having smallest font size letters representing a perfect level of clarity—referred to as 6/6 vision when read comfortably. This reflects as per the test that you are eyes are in perfect state as you can read smallest font under this test. As the letters become biggar in the rows above, corresponding to 6/9 or 6/12 vision, this mirrors how people may start facing difficulty in recognizing their abilities. Those letters further in above rows are with 6/18 or 6/24 vision begin to understand the need for corrective measures—just as self-reflection, mentorship, or life experiences can help individuals clarify their purpose and sharpen their focus.

When vision impairment reaches 6/36 or 6/60, it becomes difficult to see anything clearly. Similarly, individuals in the "84" segment lose sight of their goals and potential, lacking the focus needed to move forward.

Sachin Tendulkar's journey to greatness serves as a powerful example. His elder brother and coach, Ajit, recognized his talent and introduced him to cricket. Under the mentorship of Ramakant Achrekar, Sachin unlocked his full potential and went on to inspire millions. Even those with immense talent require guidance, vision, and clarity to achieve greatness.

Just as glasses correct physical vision, individuals in the "84" segment need metaphorical lenses to sharpen their focus and purpose. This clarity can come from self-awareness, guidance, or transformative experiences that push them toward realizing their capabilities and making a lasting impact.

These categories reflect the gradual loss and recovery of focus on the journey toward excellence.

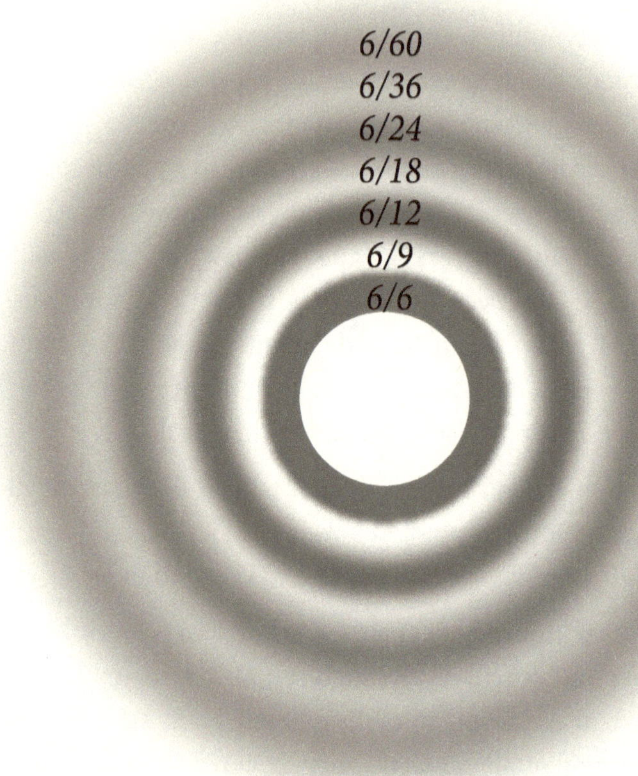

Vision Level	Focus Category	Title
6/6 Vision	Crystal Vision	Perfect clarity and focus
6/9 Vision	Focused Clarity	Minor distractions, still achieving goals
6/12 Vision	Blurred Horizons	Some ambiguity, needing refinement
6/18 Vision	Faded Focus	Noticeable decline in concentration
6/24 Vision	Distracted Vision	Significant obstacles to focus
6/36 Vision	Lost Sight	Disoriented, struggling to prioritize
6/60 Vision	Blind Spots	Severe limitations, lacking direction

These nomenclatures capture the metaphor of vision impairment, illustrating the psychological journey individuals experience as they strive toward excellence. Each step represents increasing levels of challenge and the potential for recovery through self-reflection, mentorship, and corrective actions.

Conclusion: A Call to Untie the Boat

The hidden hierarchy within society is not just about superiority; it is about awareness and intentional action. Much like the friends in the boat, many of us expend energy but never truly move forward. The key to breaking free lies in untangling ourselves from the moorings of societal norms, fear, and complacency.

The challenge is to seek clarity of vision—whether through mentorship, introspection, or deliberate practice—and to rise above the distractions that trap the majority. Only then can we embark on a journey of true progress, personal growth, and societal contribution.

Chapter 3

The Reasoning for Reluctance

Social Structures and Divisions

In every society, we live within walls shaped by rules, laws, and unspoken societal norms. These constructs—whether financial, academic, or social—act as invisible dividers, categorizing us into different "rooms" that define our worth. Money becomes a marker of success, while academic degrees serve as metrics of intelligence and credibility. However, these divisions are not a natural occurrence; they are man-made mechanisms that bestow power upon those who design and enforce them.

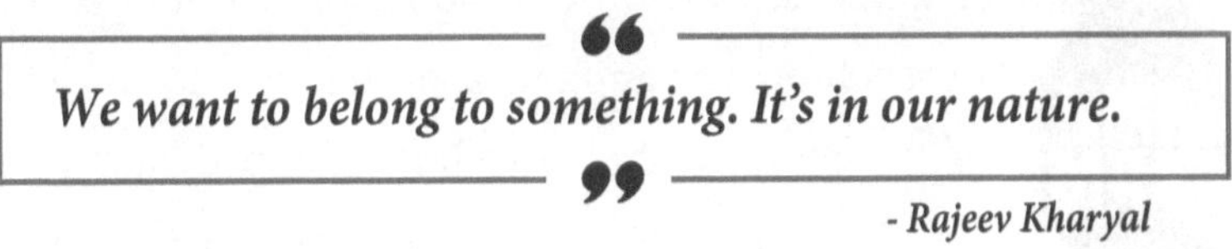

> **We want to belong to something. It's in our nature.**
>
> *- Rajeev Kharyal*

The desire to belong is not just a social craving but a primal instinct rooted in human survival. In the early days of civilization, group cooperation was essential. This fundamental need for community has shaped modern behavior, driving us to seek a sense of identity through collective affiliations

Group Psychology and the Illusion of Identity

Our identities are largely shaped by the groups we associate with—whether they be social circles, professions, or belief systems. This concept is central to group psychology, as first studied by pioneers like Gustave Le Bon, whose Group Mind Theory explains how individual ideologies are

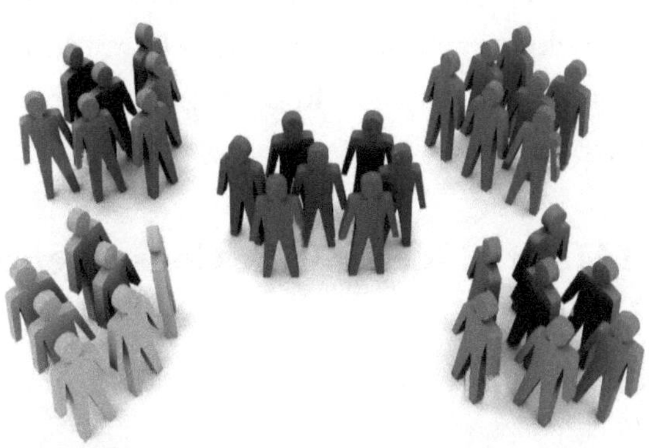

often sacrificed for the collective interest. Much like a living organism, a group takes on a life of its own, influencing its members to follow collective impulses.

A fitting analogy can be drawn from **Animal Farm** by George Orwell. The story, which starts as a fight for equality, quickly devolves into manipulation, where the pigs—representing political figures—slowly corrupt the original narrative for personal gain. Initially united in rebellion, the animals soon fall prey to the whims of the pigs, symbolizing how group dynamics can prioritize the collective's survival at the expense of individual integrity.

The Corruption of Ideals in Group Dynamics

As Orwell poignantly illustrates, those in power often manipulate language and rewrite history to maintain control. Over time, the group shifts from serving the collective good to advancing the ambitions of the few. This highlights the danger of blind allegiance to group narratives, which can transform ideals like equality into tools for exploitation.

This phenomenon mirrors Le Bon's observation that groups are prone to extremes, often driven by simplistic and exaggerated emotions. The natural desire to belong can cause individuals to overlook contradictions within their groups, leading them to conform to ideologies they might not support independently

Influence of Material Ideals & the Consequence of the Material Pursuit

Modern society's gravitation toward intense emotions and material success reflects a broader, global trend in values. Social structures worldwide, including those in the West, began with essential aspirations: securing a home, earning a living, and fulfilling basic needs. As societies evolved, however, definitions of success expanded, sometimes shifting toward outward markers of wealth and possessions.

For example, the "American Dream," rooted in the ideal of equal opportunity and social mobility, has at times become associated with material accomplishments.

The rapid spread of global media has accelerated the adoption of these ideals worldwide, reinforcing an image of success often linked to financial wealth and material accumulation. This narrative has become influential among younger generations worldwide, including Eastern Gen Z, who are in the formative stages of shaping personal values. This exposure may sometimes create tension between new aspirations and traditional values, leading to a sense of cultural disconnect.

In societies where financial success becomes a primary measure of individual worth, individuals may feel increased pressure to seek validation through material achievements and social recognition. Many find themselves in cycles of comparison, where success is measured by possessions and online approval.

When financial gain overshadows other measures of success, society's focus can drift from personal growth and meaningful accomplishments to an exclusive pursuit of wealth. While financial stability is valuable, an overemphasis on wealth can inadvertently create social divisions and detract from the pursuit of deeper, more lasting fulfillment.

> **Money is an enabler of existence, not a reason for living.**
>
> *- Rajeev Kharyal*

Unchecked materialism leads to an hollow existence. People often fall into the trap of chasing validation through possessions—luxury cars, designer clothes, and social media approval—believing these things will bring fulfillment. But in reality, this pursuit only deepens the void, creating a cycle of superficial consumption and fleeting happiness.

The Illusion of Success and Social Media's Impact

Social media, originally intended to connect people, has ironically amplified feelings of inadequacy by showcasing idealized versions of life. The constant comparison to others' curated lives distorts our perceptions of success and happiness, making us feel as though we are falling short.

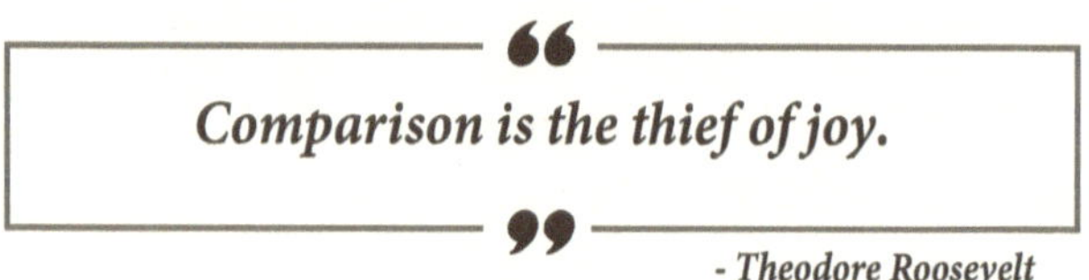

> **"**
> *Comparison is the thief of joy.*
> **"**
> *- Theodore Roosevelt*

In believing in social media's facade, we forget that it is populated by people just like ourselves—people who struggle, falter, and embellish the truth. The personas we encounter online are often exaggerated versions of reality, carefully crafted to project success and desirability. This tendency to present an idealized image creates a vicious cycle of mutual deception. Rather than focusing on building genuine character, we expend energy maintaining appearances, further distancing ourselves from authentic growth and fulfillment.

We can liken this dynamic to gold being alloyed with impurities. Just as the value of gold decreases when mixed with other metals, our sense of self diminishes when diluted by superficiality.

Attainable Gold	Adaptable Gold	The Artifical Gold
Hold its unimpacted nature	Influenced Purity for formation	

Artificial Gold

Stage 1: Creation of Faith

Something appears genuine and trustworthy, like artificial gold.

» **People believe in its authenticity.**

Stage 2: Conversion to Blind Faith

Initial faith strengthens into blind faith, with no doubts.

» **People rely on and defend its perceived value.**

Stage 3: Breach of Faith

The true nature is revealed, showing it is not what it seemed.

» **Leads to betrayal, disappointment, and loss of trust.**

In its purest form, gold is measured in carats, with 24-carat gold representing the highest level of purity. Similarly, our worth is not determined by the accumulation of material possessions or the external validation we seek, but by the integrity and depth of our character.

The Carats of Character

> **Just as gold's purity is measured in carats, a person's worth can be seen in their character. 24-carat gold is pure and rare, 23-carat is highly valued, 19-22 carat is adaptable, while 18-carat and below individuals are seen as less genuine by society.**

- Rajeev Kharyal

Pure gold is rare and valuable, not because of how it is adorned but because of its intrinsic properties—its resilience and untarnished brilliance. In the same way, we should strive for purity in our own lives, refining ourselves through meaningful experiences and authentic connections. When we strip away the distractions of materialism, we reveal the true essence of who we are—individuals of substance, whose value comes from within, not from the shine of external success.

This journey toward personal refinement mirrors the process of purifying gold. It requires time, effort, and the courage to shed superficial layers that obscure our true nature. Just as gold is purified through intense heat, we too must face challenges that test our character and strip away the illusions we hold onto. Through these efforts, we discover our inner strength, becoming the purest version of ourselves—a version that radiates, not because of external adornment, but because of the integrity we cultivate within

> **"**
>
> *A person drowned in material pursuits chooses to remain unaware of the illusion they are caught in and refuses to acknowledge reality.*
>
> **"**
>
> *- Rajeev Kharyal*

Instead of building genuine self-worth, many of us become caught in a race to meet external standards, diluting our sense of self like gold mixed with impurities. *Just as the value of gold decreases when alloyed, our self-worth diminishes when focused solely on external validation.*

Breaking Free from the Hypnosis of Materialism

Le Bon's study of group psychology likened individuals in groups to hypnotized subjects. Within these psychological groups, people often lose their sense of individual responsibility, acting without clear thought or analysis. When it comes to materialism, this "group-think" is fueled by society's collective obsession with financial gain and status symbols.

To fully escape societal pressure, we must look beyond social media and similar platforms. It is equally important to examine the influence of institutions like workplaces, schools, and other environments that perpetuate misconceptions about intelligence and success.

Chapter 4

The Myth of Smartness

> **The more laws and order are made prominent, the more thieves and robbers there will be**
>
> –Lao Tzu

Understanding the Illusion

We've discussed how many people feel lost, unaware of the paths they walk because they've unknowingly given up their power. But how did this happen? How did society create this invisible control?

One way to understand this is through the social contract theory. It suggests that people agree to give up some freedoms in exchange for social order and protection. We agree to follow laws and rules to ensure safety and fairness for everyone.

However, in the process of creating a structured society, we sometimes sacrifice more than we realize. Our individual freedom—the idea that we shouldn't be controlled—clashes with the need for rules. While rules protect us from chaos, they also limit us, creating a world where we may be unknowingly controlled by others.

Take, for example, the finance sector. Rules like anti-monopoly laws and consumer protection measures prevent big companies from exploiting people. But people often feel powerless, realizing that they've traded too much freedom for the promise of stability.

In this balance between personal freedom and societal rules, the myth of "smartness" emerges. Society starts to dictate what it means to be intelligent and successful, making it hard for individuals to define those terms for themselves.

Western Ideologies and Global Narratives

To understand why many people feel constrained by traditional definitions of intelligence and success, it's helpful to consider the influence of global narratives, including Western ideals, on these perceptions. Over time, certain Western concepts of material success and intelligence have contributed to shaping societal standards of worth worldwide.

The "American Dream," for instance, originally celebrated ideals of equal opportunity and social mobility. Yet, as this idea has evolved, it has sometimes taken on more materialistic undertones, where wealth and power are prominent markers of success. Through media and popular culture, these ideals have spread beyond the West, influencing societies worldwide. This has led some individuals to prioritize material achievements and outward success as key indicators of intelligence and accomplishment.

These global narratives have also influenced educational systems, which often prioritize test scores and academic performance over fostering a love of learning and diverse skill development. In many cases, intelligence is measured primarily through standardized testing and academic achievements, while qualities such as creativity, emotional intelligence, and practical skills are undervalued

Cultural Representation: 3 Idiots

The effects of these ideals are perfectly captured in the movie 3 Idiots, a popular Indian film that critiques the rigid and outdated notions of success in education. The film's protagonist, Rancho, represents a student who values creativity and practical knowledge over rote memorization and grades. His unorthodox approach to learning leads to happiness and success, even though the system initially tries to suppress his way of thinking.

In contrast, Chatur, a classmate who focuses entirely on memorization and test scores, faces embarrassment when his lack of true understanding is exposed. In one scene, Chatur delivers a speech filled with incorrect phrases, unaware of the meaning behind the words he recites. This highlights how an overemphasis on grades and memorization can leave individuals unprepared for real-life challenges.

This film resonates with many students today who feel pressured to meet unrealistic academic standards. The societal expectation to "perform better than your peers" has turned genuine competition into a race for superficial validation, where true learning and curiosity are sacrificed.

The Consequences of Chasing External Validation & The Illusion of Smartness

The pursuit of academic excellence, as defined by traditional standards, has created a generation of individuals who measure their worth based on external validation. Instead of focusing on personal growth, many students feel compelled to chase high test scores, prestigious degrees, and societal approval.

This has led to a culture where students are viewed as products, moving through a factory-like system of coaching centers and exam prep courses. The focus on securing top marks and landing high-paying jobs overshadows the importance of curiosity, creativity, and passion.

Over time, this pressure creates an environment where students feel trapped, conforming to societal expectations rather than pursuing their own interests. Schools and universities become places where obedience is valued more than innovation, and students are discouraged from thinking outside the box.

This narrow view of intelligence, focused on financial success and academic accolades, reinforces the myth of smartness. Many people start equating intelligence with material gain, believing that being *"smart" means earning more money, owning more possessions, and gaining more social status.*

But this view ignores the true complexity of human intelligence. Qualities like emotional intelligence, adaptability, creativity, and resilience are just as important—if not more so—than IQ or academic success.

One of the reasons IQ tests often fail to measure true intelligence is that they focus too much on specific cognitive skills. In a study led by Adam Hampshire at the Brain and Mind Institute, researchers found that IQ tests don't fully capture a person's intelligence. They discovered that intelligence isn't a single quality, but rather a combination of memory, reasoning, and verbal skills. This more comprehensive view highlights the limitations of traditional measures of intelligence.

The fixation on IQ and grades can lead people to overlook their own potential. The belief that intelligence is something that can be ranked with numbers or scores blinds us to the diverse strengths that each person brings to the table.

Breaking Free from the Myth & Pursuing True Excellence

So, how do we break free from the myth of smartness? First, we must challenge the societal norms that define intelligence and success by narrow standards. It requires us to recognize the multifaceted nature of intelligence and to value qualities like empathy, creativity, and resilience as much as traditional cognitive skills.

To break out of the trap of external validation, we need to shift our focus inward. Pursuing personal growth, passion, and purpose is far more rewarding than seeking approval from others. This process involves questioning societal expectations, embracing uncertainty, and being willing to step outside the box.

It also requires taking practical steps. Limiting time spent on social media, seeking out mentors who value personal development, and cultivating emotional intelligence are ways we can realign our lives with what truly matters.

True excellence isn't about meeting society's predefined standards. It's about pursuing what you love, learning from your mistakes, and growing as an individual. It's about embracing lifelong learning and focusing on the qualities that make us truly human—our ability to connect, to innovate, and to grow.

By rejecting the narrow definitions of intelligence that society has imposed on us, we open ourselves up to a world of possibilities. Instead of striving for external success, we can focus on personal fulfillment, creating a life that reflects our values and aspirations.

In the end, true intelligence lies not in what we know or what we own, but in how we live, how we grow, and how we contribute to the world around us

Chapter 5

Elevating from the Majority

To rise above the ordinary requires not only motivation but a proactive approach. The journey to reaching greater heights, like Segment 13, demands focus and persistence. One individual who truly embodies this journey is Dr. APJ Abdul Kalam, whose story has left a lasting impression on me.

Inspiration from Dr. APJ Abdul Kalam

Dr. Kalam's life began in the small town of Rameswaram in Tamil Nadu, where he faced financial hardship. His father was a boat owner and the local mosque's Imam, earning a modest living by ferrying pilgrims. Despite these challenges, Dr. Kalam was unwavering in his commitment to education. He didn't chase material wealth; instead, he sought excellence through knowledge and purpose.

Dr. Kalam played a pivotal role in India's missile development program, earning him the title "Missile Man of India." He later became the President of India, a role he used to champion youth empowerment, education, and national development. His vision for India's future inspired millions.

However, Dr. Kalam's goal was never just to escape poverty or accumulate wealth. He aimed for true excellence with a clear vision, and the material perks he earned were simply by-products of his pursuit, not his main objective. His story teaches us that reaching a stage like Segment 13 requires more than just material privilege—it requires strength, perseverance, and a deep understanding of one's goals.

The Hero's Journey: A Universal Path of Growth

Throughout history, the concept of the "hero's journey" has appeared in various cultures. This journey represents a path filled with challenges, transformation, and personal growth. One such story that perfectly illustrates this journey is that of Arjuna in the Mahabharata.

Arjuna, one of the Pandava brothers, faced many obstacles—moral dilemmas, personal conflicts, and societal

expectations. One of his most significant moments occurred on the battlefield of Kurukshetra, where he struggled with the idea of fighting his own family. This inner conflict is a reflection of the larger struggle many of us face when trying to align our duties with our inner values.

Through his dialogue with Lord Krishna in the Bhagavad Gita, Arjuna finds clarity about his purpose. He learns that true wisdom lies in balancing action with inner peace.

Krishna's words,

> **66**
> *Those who see action in inaction and inaction in action are truly wise among humans*
> **99**

resonate deeply, highlighting the importance of understanding when to act and when to pause.

Like Arjuna, we all face moments where we question our path. It's through self-reflection, courage, and wisdom that we can find our purpose and take the necessary steps to move forward.

I remember a story from my childhood about a farmer searching for water for his crops. After digging to 30 feet and finding nothing, he didn't give up. He continued to 100 feet, then 250 feet, 500 feet, and even 750 feet until he finally struck water. His determination paid off, and his crops flourished.

This farmer's persistence mirrors the journey to excellence. Whether we are striving to achieve success like Dr. APJ Abdul Kalam or facing internal struggles like Arjuna, we must keep going, even when progress feels slow or uncertain. Comparing our journey to others only distracts us. Like the farmer, we need to understand our unique challenges and dig deep, knowing that success comes with perseverance.

Conforming to Norms and the Struggle for Authenticity

From a young age, society pressures us to conform to its definitions of what is "normal" or acceptable. We're often taught—both directly and indirectly—that fitting in requires suppressing our unique qualities. Even as children, we learn that defying these expectations has consequences.

I vividly recall one of my first experiences with this pressure to conform. Naturally left-handed, I was encouraged by my teacher to write with my right hand. It was a quiet but clear message: "Be someone else to fit in." Although this may seem minor, looking back, I see how it set a pattern of compromising my authentic self to meet external expectations.

Over time, I found it increasingly difficult to be my true self, feeling consumed by the need to present a persona that matched what others wanted to see. Many of us experience this throughout life—adjusting ourselves to fit a mold. Small compromises may seem insignificant at first, but they can snowball into larger patterns of behavior that distance us from our authentic selves.

It's not just about societal definitions of success or status symbols. Conformity can creep into every aspect of life, from the way we express ourselves to the goals we pursue. And even after achieving what society tells us will bring happiness—financial success, career milestones, social recognition—many of us still feel an inner void, realizing that we've strayed from our true path.

Breaking Free: Pursuing True Excellence

There's nothing inherently wrong with pursuing material success. It can be a valuable marker of achievement. But to rise above the majority, we must recognize that material success alone cannot provide lasting fulfilment. Many people achieve external success but still lack the intellectual freedom to break free from societal narratives.

For instance, uneducated parents who give their children the freedom to explore often witness remarkable success in their children's lives. Without the burden of societal expectations, these children follow their passions, often excelling in ways that predefined paths cannot anticipate. Many go on to achieve great things—clearing entrance exams, joining prestigious institutions, and contributing to society in unique ways.

To truly elevate from the majority, we must balance material achievements with a deeper sense of purpose, allowing ourselves the intellectual freedom to grow, question, and challenge the narratives we've been given.

Navigating Complex Systems

The journey from the majority (Segment 84) to a higher level (Segment 13) has become more complex in today's world. What was once a simpler path is now influenced by modern societal, educational, and economic challenges, making progress slower and more demanding. To succeed in navigating these systems, one must show conscious effort, persistence, and the ability to adapt.

Yet, as examples like Sachin Tendulkar and Dr. APJ Abdul Kalam demonstrate, this transition is achievable. Tendulkar turned his passion and raw talent into unmatched success by practicing relentlessly, staying focused, and overcoming difficulties. Similarly, Dr. Kalam rose from humble beginnings to become an icon of innovation and leadership, fueled by his commitment to learning and his drive to make a difference. Their lives remind us that challenges can be overcome with dedication, resilience, and purposeful action.

As we move forward in our own journeys, we should keep the 3Es in mind: Experience, Express, and Evolve. Life's experiences—whether they bring joy or teach tough lessons—help us grow and understand the world around us. By expressing ourselves—through words, creativity, or actions—we contribute uniquely to the world. Finally, by evolving, we adapt and progress, continually becoming better versions of ourselves. The 3Es remind us that ***our purpose is not just to exist but to actively engage, learn, and improve throughout life's journey.***

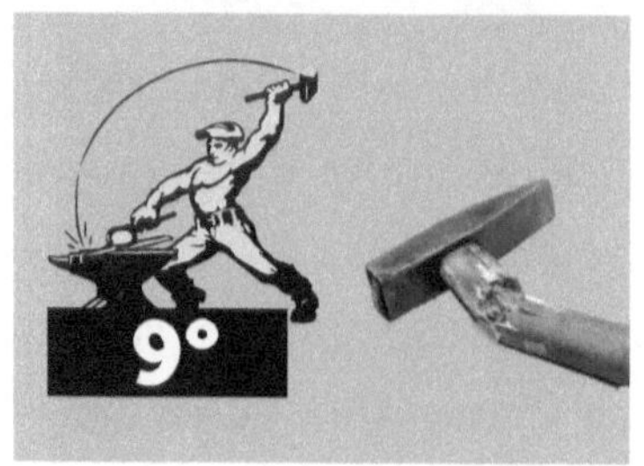

The Iron Metaphor:
Transformation through Effort

To understand this process of transition more deeply, think of iron. In its cold state, iron is rigid and unchanging, much like the challenges we face when we don't put in enough effort to overcome them. However, when iron is heated, it can be shaped into useful forms—this is similar to how persistence and effort allow us to mold our challenges into opportunities.

For more complex problems, iron must be heated to an even higher temperature—over 999 degrees Celsius—before it becomes molten and can be poured into a mold. This process represents the most challenging obstacles in life, which require sustained effort and focus to fully overcome.

By putting in the work, staying focused, and persisting through obstacles, we can transform ourselves and our lives, just as iron can be reshaped through heat and effort.

The Path Ahead: Self-Awareness and Social Awareness

As we reflect on the stories of strength and perseverance we've encountered, it becomes clear that personal and social awareness are crucial. Self-awareness allows us to understand our unique challenges, while social awareness helps us navigate the complex systems that shape our lives.

The journey to Segment 13 is not just about material success or societal validation. It's about understanding ourselves, pursuing true excellence, and overcoming the obstacles that stand in our way. By cultivating persistence, authenticity, and intellectual freedom, we can elevate ourselves from the majority and embark on a path of genuine personal growth.

The Heat of Transformation

66

Iron remains unchanged until it's heated and shaped. Similarly, life's challenges only change with focused effort, and critical problems require utmost attention and continued efforts until a breakthrough solution is achieved.

99

- Rajeev Kharyal

Section-A
Summary
(Chapters 1-5)

Societal Division Framework: This section introduces an analytical framework revealing society divisions into three groups: the '3', the '13', and the '84'. These groups represent varying levels of awareness, influence, and impact, providing a perspective on both individual and collective consciousness.

The '84' encompasses the majority, who are often immersed in the routine of daily life. The narrative explores how the majority is systematically conditioned from a young age. The educational system prioritizes rote learning and standardized testing over creativity and critical thinking, creating a narrow definition of intelligence. Media reinforces societal constructs by shaping perceptions of success, beauty, intelligence, and worth, often glorifying material success and external validation. As a result, this group remains largely unaware of the societal structures that influence their lives, limiting their potential for self-awareness and personal growth.

The 'Hidden Divide': A key concept, the 'hidden divide', represents the psychological and social forces that perpetuate these divisions. Group dynamics, the need for belonging, and dominant societal narratives reinforce the split between the '84', '13', and '3'. The narrative discussed critiques the prevailing definition of intelligence, which is often measured by IQ tests and academic achievements. Cultural narratives emphasize financial prosperity and professional status, limiting the vision of personal achievement and fostering competition.

Transitioning from the '84' to the '13' is portrayed as a journey of heightened awareness and personal growth. This transformation requires courage, self-reflection, and a willingness to challenge societal norms. The journey is likened to the hero's journey, emphasizing the challenges and rewards of breaking free from societal constraints. It calls for a re-evaluation of societal pressures to conform and advocate for pursuing true excellence rooted in individual passions and values. Breaking free from societal constructs and seeking genuine personal growth is framed as a path to transcending the limitations of the '84'. This pursuit is seen as a radical act of reclaiming one's agency and redefining success on personal terms.

Cultural and Philosophical Enrichment: The narrative is enriched with cultural references, personal anecdotes, and philosophical concepts that deepen the exploration of societal divisions and personal transformation. Readers are encouraged to examine their own positions within these societal structures and consider pathways to greater awareness, fulfillment, and potential.

Conclusion: These chapters lay the groundwork for understanding societal divisions and the potential for individual transformation. Through philosophical insights, personal reflections, and cultural critiques, readers are invited to critically examine their place in society and pursue a path of personal excellence and heightened awareness.

Chapter 6

Elevating from the Majority

Johann Wolfgang von Goethe once said,

> **66**
>
> ***Self-knowledge comes from knowing other people.***
>
> **99**

This statement captures the essence of self-awareness: understanding ourselves by recognizing how we interact with and relate to others.

Self-awareness is the ability to recognize and understand our emotions, motivations, thoughts, and desires. It's about knowing what makes you unique and being aware of your values, strengths, and weaknesses. There are two types of self-awareness:

1.**Internal Self-Awareness:** This is understanding your own values, strengths, weaknesses, and moral compass.

2.**External Self-Awareness:** This is the awareness of how others perceive you and how your actions impact them.

The Power of Self-Awareness

Mahatma Gandhi's life is a profound example of self-awareness. Known worldwide for his philosophy of non-violence and peaceful protest, Gandhi was deeply aware of his own imperfections. In his autobiography, The Story of My Experiments with Truth, he openly discusses his struggles with anger, desire, and personal weaknesses.

He wrote,

> **66**
>
> ***I realized that the same soul lives in all of us and that all human beings are equal. It is possible for each one of us to attain the same measure of divine perfection.***
>
> **99**
>
> *Mahatma Gandhi's*

This reflection reveals his deep internal self-awareness and his ongoing journey toward personal growth and self-improvement.

Think about a time when you faced a personal challenge or inner struggle. How did self-awareness—or a lack of it—affect your response to the situation? Reflecting on such moments can help you identify areas where you might develop a deeper understanding of yourself.

The Pareto Principle and Self-Awareness

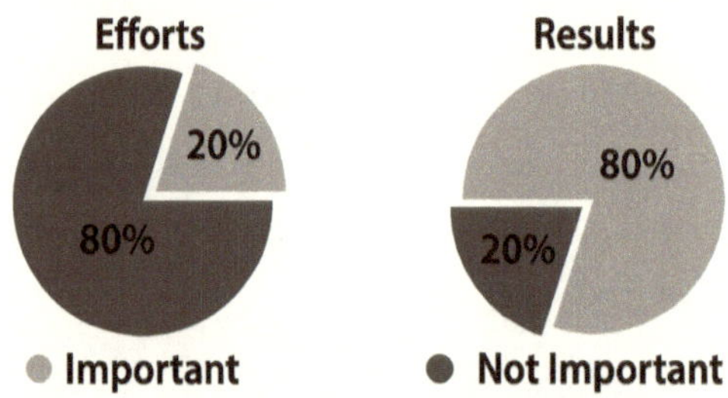

The Pareto Principle, also known as the 80/20 Rule, states that 80% of results often come from 20% of efforts. This principle is commonly used in productivity and business, but it also applies to personal growth. Focusing on key areas of self-awareness can lead to the most significant improvements in your life. On the other hand, focusing too much on less impactful behaviors may only result in minimal progress.

For example, if you recognize that a lack of patience is a significant obstacle in your personal relationships, working on this one trait might lead to a major improvement in how you interact with others. Understanding where your efforts will have the most impact is essential for personal growth.

The Gap in Segment 84

People in Segment 84 often wonder why they think and act the way they do, but struggle to find clear answers. This is largely due to a lack of deep self-awareness. Without fully understanding their motivations, actions, and how their thoughts align with their goals, it becomes difficult for them to progress.

Self-awareness theory, introduced by Duval and Wicklund in 1972, explains that when we engage in self-reflection, we compare our actions with our internal goals. If we notice a gap between where we are and where we want to be, it motivates us to change and grow. But without self-awareness, this gap remains unnoticed, and growth stalls.

Consider running a business where you have all the technical skills needed to succeed but lack Emotional Intelligence (EQ). Without the ability to manage your emotions or relate to others, your business might struggle despite your technical expertise. *EQ is critical for understanding both yourself and the people around you, enabling smoother interactions and better decision-making.*

Take a moment to reflect: In what areas of your life do you see a gap between your actions and your goals? Is there a personal trait or behavior that might be holding you back from achieving the success you want?

EQ: The Key to Success

Warren G. Bennis, a leadership expert, once said,

> *Emotional intelligence, more than anything else—more than IQ or expertise—accounts for 85% to 90% of success at work. IQ is important, but it doesn't make you stand out. Emotional intelligence can.*

Emotional Quotient (EQ) is the ability to understand and manage your emotions and those of others. While IQ focuses on cognitive abilities, EQ is about building meaningful connections and understanding the emotions that drive human behavior. This is what truly sets people apart in personal and professional settings.

For example, a leader with high EQ can inspire their team, manage conflicts effectively, and create an environment of trust. This goes beyond problem-solving—it's about understanding what motivates people and helping them achieve their best potential.

Beyond Helping Others

Emotional intelligence goes beyond just helping others. It's about understanding the unique strengths and emotions of those around you and aligning your goals with theirs. When you understand the motivations of your colleagues, friends, or employees, you can create an environment where everyone thrives.

Take Dr. Devi Shetty, the founder of Narayana Health. Dr. Shetty didn't just focus on treating his patients' physical health; he understood the emotional and financial burdens they faced. His ability to empathize with both his staff and patients allowed him to create a healthcare system that serves people from all walks of life. His leadership is an example of how emotional intelligence and social awareness can lead to greater success and societal impact.

Social Awareness: The Key to Connection

While self-awareness helps you understand your own emotions, social awareness is what enables you to connect with others. It's about recognizing social cues, empathizing with people from different backgrounds, and building strong relationships. Social awareness allows you to understand how others see the world, which can help you navigate complex social situations more effectively.

Khan Sir, a famous teacher from Patna, is an excellent example of someone who used social awareness to make a difference. He recognized the financial struggles faced by students from poor families and created affordable coaching classes to help them succeed. His ability to understand his students' challenges set him apart, showing how social awareness can lead to practical solutions that benefit everyone.

Emotional Availability: A Foundation for Trust

Joel Frank, a clinical psychologist, explains that emotional availability is about being open to understanding and sharing the emotions of others. It's more than just being physically present—it's about forming deep emotional connections and being available to receive the emotions of those around you.

Dr. Kiran Bedi, India's first female IPS officer, exemplifies emotional availability in her leadership. In her efforts to reform Tihar Jail, Dr. Bedi introduced programs that focused on emotional and mental growth, not just punishment. She treated prisoners with dignity, helping them reintegrate into society in positive ways. Her leadership in law enforcement showed that emotional availability can transform institutions and build trust between people and systems.

This openness to emotional connections can also be seen in personal relationships. For example, think about a time when you felt deeply understood and supported by someone you care about. That emotional connection likely helped you feel valued and strengthened your relationship.

Bridging the gap Between segments 84 and 13

To bridge the gap between Segments 84 and 13, self-awareness alone isn't enough. It must be combined with social awareness and emotional intelligence. Understanding your own emotions is the first step, but connecting those insights with how others feel and think is what truly leads to growth.

When these two aspects come together, you develop a deeper Emotional Intelligence (EQ), which helps you build meaningful connections, foster strong relationships, and create an environment where you and those around you can thrive.

Chapter 7

The Power of Emotions

> *Continuous improvement is better than delayed perfection.*
>
> -Mark Twain

Emotional intelligence (EQ) has become an important part of how we understand and interact with others. It plays a big role in both personal relationships and at work, showing how useful it is everywhere. This is what makes the 13 segment stand out, as we discussed earlier.

The Growth of Emotional Quotient (EQ)

The idea of EQ started in academic discussions when PhD student Wayne Payne mentioned it in his 1985 dissertation. Later, in 1990, psychologists Peter Salovey and John Mayer published a key article about EQ. But it was Daniel Goleman's 1995 book, *Emotional Intelligence: Why It Can Matter More Than IQ,* that made EQ popular and brought it into everyday conversations. Goleman's work showed how important EQ is for success in both personal life and at work.

Even though EQ was first talked about by scholars, its roots are connected to our basic human need to grow, improve ourselves, and live peacefully with others.

From History to Sacred Epic

Emotional Quotient (EQ) is not a new idea; it has deep roots in history and culture.

For example, during the Champaran Satyagraha in 1917, Mahatma Gandhi helped indigo farmers who were being mistreated by British landowners. Gandhi understood the farmers' struggles and took the time to investigate their living conditions. By living with them and understanding their problems, he gained their trust and encouraged them to fight for justice.

This shows how important it is to understand people's emotions and build connections, which helped bring the farmers together to demand their rights.

EQ is also found in ancient wisdom. In Indian mythology, the Mahabharata offers many lessons on emotional intelligence. The characters face difficult situations where they need to understand and manage their emotions to maintain personal integrity and social harmony.

One key figure, Vidura, was a wise royal advisor who showed strong emotional intelligence. During the conflict between the Pandavas and Kauravas, Vidura tried to mediate and prevent war by using his wisdom and empathy. He stayed calm and gave advice based on what was right (dharma), even though his advice was often ignored by the Kauravas, especially Duryodhana.

A great example of Vidura's emotional intelligence was when he warned King Dhritarashtra to stop the war. Although he was close to both sides, Vidura remained neutral and focused on the greater good. He spoke up bravely about the dangers of Duryodhana's greed and ambition. Vidura's ability to stay calm, understand others' feelings, and stay true to his values shows high emotional Quotient.

Vidura's story shows that EQ is not just about controlling your own emotions but also about guiding others with empathy, wisdom, and integrity.

The Science of Emotions

To understand EQ better, we need to know how emotions work. Everything in our bodies happens for a reason, and emotions are a key part of how we see the world. Even though emotions seem hard to touch, they actually come from chemicals released in the brain. For example, happiness is linked to chemicals like serotonin and dopamine, while stress is connected to a chemical called cortisol. These chemicals help us understand ourselves and what's happening around us.

If we think of everything around us as information, emotions help us focus on the most important details and adjust to changes. For example, when someone faces danger, fear triggers a quick "fight-or-flight" reaction, helping them respond appropriately. This is why understanding EQ is important, especially when growing from segment 84 to segment 13.

As Charles Darwin said:

> **It is not the strongest or smartest who survive, but those who can adapt to change.**
>
> *-Charles Darwin*

Understanding Emotional Barriers

EQ is important, but many of us struggle to develop it. There are different reasons for this, including barriers we create ourselves or ones caused by others. For example, past trauma can make people suppress their emotions, blocking their emotional growth. These barriers can distort how we see the world, making it harder to trust our own judgment. Social factors, like our environment and relationships, also affect how we feel and express emotions.

We have the powerful story of Arunima Sinha, the first female amputee to climb Mount Everest. After losing her leg in a train accident, Arunima could have let grief take over. Instead, she used her emotional strength to achieve an incredible goal: climbing Mount Everest. Her journey shows how EQ—especially managing fear and pain—can lead to amazing achievements. Arunima's story is a lesson in resilience, emotional control, and turning hardship into success

Story reminds us that emotional Quotient isn't just about understanding emotions. It's about learning to manage them in ways that help us take meaningful action. By mastering this, we can move beyond reactive emotions and make better decisions.

Arunima Sinha story connect to the biological side of emotions, like the release of cortisol (a stress hormone) during tough times. This hormone can cloud our thinking, making it hard to respond clearly. By understanding how these emotional barriers form—whether through chemicals, our minds, or society—we can learn to break them down and become more emotionally aware and empowered

Identifying Barriers to Emotional Intelligence (EQ)

Although emotional intelligence (EQ) is important, many of us struggle to develop it. This happens because of barriers created by ourselves or others. These barriers make us see things in a distorted way, affecting our judgment and making us doubt our abilities. Social factors, like the people around us and how we interact, also play a big role in shaping how we handle and express our emotions.

These barriers come from both inside and outside of us. Internally, our fears, insecurities, and past experiences can stop us from growing emotionally. Externally, society and cultural expectations can pressure us to act in certain ways that don't match how we really feel. This creates a big challenge in building true emotional intelligence.

To develop EQ, we need to understand these barriers and make an effort to overcome them. By recognizing these pressures and working through them, we can align our true emotions with how we express them, leading to more honest and meaningful relationships

The Tata Family's Legacy of Emotional Intelligence

To overcome barriers to emotional intelligence, it's important to understand emotions and express them in a healthy, honest way.

The leadership of the Tata Group, from its founder **J.N. Tata** to the current **CEO N. Chandrasekaran,** reflects a deep-rooted commitment to emotional Quotient (EQ). Each leader in the Tata legacy has demonstrated empathy, social responsibility, and a focus on the well-being of employees and society. Below, we explore the EQ challenges faced by each leader and how they navigated them:

J.N. Tata (Founder):

Jamsetji Tata founded the Tata Group on compassion and social responsibility. His biggest challenge came while building India's first steel plant, facing opposition from British industrialists and skepticism from the Indian business community. Despite these barriers, he prioritized employee welfare, providing housing, healthcare, and education to workers—an extraordinary move at the time. His ability to focus on the long-term welfare of his people showcased his emotional intelligence, laying the foundation for future Tata leadership.

J.R.D. Tata:

J.R.D. Tata expanded on his grandfather's vision by making employee satisfaction central to the company's success. His leadership was tested when Air India transitioned from private ownership to nationalization. Despite the external pressures, J.R.D. maintained a strong focus on employee well-being, personally engaging with staff to build trust and loyalty. His hands-on approach and unwavering commitment to excellence reflected his deep emotional intelligence, which helped Air India maintain a culture of quality even during turbulent times.

Ratan Tata:

Ratan Tata's exceptional emotional intelligence (EQ) has been a cornerstone of his leadership, especially during challenging times when the reputation of his companies and the well-being of his employees were at stake.

One example of his EQ was during the launch of the Tata Nano, a car aimed at making transportation affordable for Indian families. Despite initial excitement, the Nano faced criticism due to production delays, safety concerns, and public ridicule. Instead of reacting defensively, Ratan Tata listened to customer feedback, improved the product, and ensured safety standards were met, reaffirming his commitment to providing affordable yet reliable transportation.

Similarly, during Tata Group's acquisition of Jaguar Land Rover (JLR) in 2008, Ratan Tata demonstrated resilience and empathy. The acquisition, made during a financial crisis, raised concerns among JLR employees. By transparently addressing their anxieties and allowing the brands autonomy to innovate, he built trust and confidence. This approach led to one of the automotive industry's most remarkable turnarounds, with JLR achieving significant success in subsequent years.

The most profound demonstration of Ratan Tata's emotional intelligence, however, was seen in the aftermath of the 26/11 Mumbai terrorist attacks. Following the tragedy at the Taj Mahal Palace Hotel, Ratan Tata personally visited and supported the families of affected employees. His swift actions included financial aid, counseling, and ongoing assistance, showcasing a deep sense of empathy and responsibility. This unparalleled compassion deeply resonated with people across India, solidifying his legacy as a leader who prioritizes humanity over business.

Ratan Tata's EQ-driven leadership exemplifies the power of empathy and integrity, leaving an indelible mark on his employees, stakeholders, and society.

Noel Tata (Chairman of Tata Trusts): Noel Tata, known for his quiet but effective leadership, played a key role in expanding Tata Group internationally, particularly through Tata International and Tata Trent. His challenge was ensuring that Tata's values of empathy and social responsibility were upheld while expanding in new, diverse markets. Noel's emotional intelligence helped him build trust with international partners and employees, emphasizing long-term relationships and a people-centered approach. His calm demeanor and focus on relationships strengthened Tata's global presence.

N. Chandrasekaran (Current CEO): N. Chandrasekaran faced a significant challenge during the COVID-19 pandemic, where balancing business operations with employee safety and social responsibility was crucial. Under his leadership, Tata Group quickly launched relief efforts, including setting up healthcare facilities and supporting vaccine development. Chandrasekaran's emotional intelligence was evident in his calm, empathetic approach, ensuring the well-being of employees and communities, while also keeping the business resilient during an unprecedented global crisis.

Each Tata leader faced real-world challenges where their emotional Quotient not only helped overcome obstacles but also reinforced the company's enduring values of empathy, social responsibility, and care for the community.

Guna Harmony Index & its analogy

The core idea of the scale is rooted in Hindu astrology's **"36 Gunas"**, which determine the compatibility between partners. The higher the number of matching gunas, the better the relationship's chances of success. This scale mirrors that concept, translating it into a practical tool for evaluating modern relationships, allowing individuals to reflect on the emotional and psychological aspects of their connections.

Relationship Insights

> **66**
>
> *Evaluate your core relationships on a scale from soulmate to conflicting (i.e. from 36 to 14 Guna in astrology) to gain insights and encourage continuous emotional growth. Strive to move beyond conflict and compromise, aiming for a happier and more fulfilling life.*
>
> **99**
>
> *– Rajeev Kharyal*

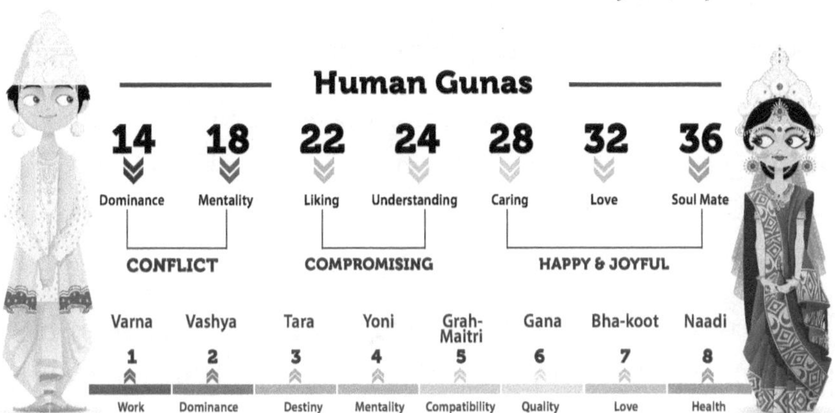

Think of the Guna Harmony Index like climbing a mountain.

At the bottom (14), you're in the foothills, where the terrain is rough and the path is full of challenges, symbolizing a relationship focused on power struggles or control. As you ascend, you reach different stages: mentality (18) represents the mental alignment needed for the journey, liking (22) reflects a bond built on trust and affection, and understanding (24) is where you're able to recognize each other's needs.

Moving higher, caring (28) is when you start taking care of each other, while love (32) represents reaching the summit, where you cherish and support each other fully.

Soulmate (36) is the peak – the ultimate view – where emotional, intellectual, and spiritual unity creates a profound connection.

Significance for Self-Reflection:

The Guna Harmony Index encourages individuals to continuously strive to improve their relationships, whether they are at a low score of 14 or a higher score like 28 or 32. It is a dynamic tool meant for growth, showing that relationships evolve and can improve with effort, emotional intelligence, and mutual understanding. It ties emotional intelligence with relationship growth, promoting self-awareness, social awareness, and emotional regulation as critical tools for creating healthier connections.

Self-awareness involves recognizing where you and your relationship fall on the scale, identifying your emotional strengths and weaknesses. Social awareness helps you understand your partner's needs, desires, and feelings, which is crucial for fostering deeper connections.

The goal is not just to reach the highest point on the scale, but to continuously evolve, recognize weaknesses, and work towards creating a mutually satisfying and balanced relationship.

Effective Communication

> **For effective communication, Choose your words carefully, but remember that their combination with tone and body language makes the highest impact.**
>
> *– Rajeev Kharyal*

For effective communication among leaders, colleagues, and family members, attention must be given to the following:

1. Selection of words that convey the intended emotions in a message.

2. Variation in the tonality of voice to express the emotional nuance.

3. Effective use of facial expressions to reinforce the emotions being communicated.

This awareness allows us to adapt our communication method based on the criticality and importance of the message. The three modes of communication to consider are:

1. Text Communication

Words only: This mode conveys factual information but misses non-verbal cues like tone and facial expressions. It often leads to misunderstandings when emotions are critical to the message.

2. Phone Call Communication

Words + Vocal Tone: Here, you add tone and emotion, making the message clearer and allowing the receiver to understand the emotional context better than with just text.

3. In-Person Communication

Words + Vocal Tone + Body Language: The most complete form of communication where words, tone, and non-verbal cues (facial expressions, gestures, eye contact) combine to express the full emotional depth.

Albert Mehrabian's research underscores The power of non-verbal communication.

According to him, when a person communicates feelings, three elements—words, tone of voice, and facial expression—contribute differently to how others perceive and like the person. Specifically, words account for

7% of message pertaining to feelings and attitudes is in the words that are spoken.

38% of message pertaining to feelings and attitudes is the way the words are said.

55% of message pertaining to feelings and attitudes is in facial

This highlights the necessity of in-person interactions, where all three channels of communication can work together effectively.

Dr. Reuven Bar

On's model of emotional intelligence provides a detailed framework for understanding how emotional and social competencies are inter-related and contribute to overall well-being. His model covers various aspects of emotional intelligence, including intrapersonal skills, interpersonal skills, adaptability, stress management, and general mood. By explaining these components, Bar-On offers a comprehensive view of emotional intelligence, highlighting its complex nature and the importance of each dimension in nurturing emotional mastery.

A great example of EQ in action is **Nelson Mandela,** the famous South African leader. During his 27 years in prison, Mandela showed incredible self-control and empathy. Instead of becoming bitter or angry at his oppressors, he tried to understand their point of view. This helped him lead South Africa through a peaceful  transition from apartheid to democracy. Mandela's ability to manage his emotions and inspire others shows how emotional intelligence can bring positive change and unity

When Emotions Come to Life

Popular culture can help us understand complex ideas like emotional intelligence. A great example is Pixar's 2015 animated movie Inside Out, which explores emotions in a fun and imaginative way.

Although I don't usually watch animated movies, my daughter convinced me to see it, and we spent an evening discussing how relatable it was.

The movie shows how emotions shape the thoughts and actions of Riley, an 11-year-old girl, by bringing her emotions to life as characters: Joy, Sadness, Anger, Fear, and Disgust. It explores how these emotions affect Riley's behavior, especially when her family moves to a new city. At first, Joy tries to keep Riley happy all the time and pushes Sadness away, but this leads to emotional imbalance. As the story progresses, Joy learns that Sadness is just as important for Riley's well-being. For example, when Riley feels homesick, it is Sadness that helps her reconnect with her parents, showing the value of being emotionally honest.

Inside Out teaches us about emotional intelligence (EQ) by showing the importance of recognizing and valuing all our emotions. The film highlights how emotions work together and how managing them can help us grow, solve problems, and build stronger relationships. By understanding and controlling our emotions, we can lead happier, more meaningful lives. This idea connects to the human desire for self-improvement and living in harmony with others.

Understanding Emotional Quotient in Simple Terms

Humans have always wanted to improve themselves. In the early days, this was mainly about survival—finding food, shelter, and staying safe. But as people started living together in groups, they realized that getting along with others was just as important. They learned how to work together, communicate well, and share resources to survive as a group. These behaviors helped build peaceful communities, which was essential for everyone's wellbeing.

Emotional Quotient is simply the ability to understand and manage our own emotions and recognize the feelings of others. This helps us communicate better, handle conflicts, and build stronger relationships Throughout history, people have used it to overcome difficulties and inspire those around them. It's real power is in how we use it in everyday life. It helps us navigate challenges and contribute positively to society.

Chapter 8

Intent in Action

> *When your intention is noble and strong.*
> *You can't be defeated.*
>
> -Maharana Pratap

The immediate response one has after analysing the Gunas Scale can be categorised into 2 ways: action (actively addressing the findings and implementing changes) or inaction (choosing not to address the insights received). When confronted with the harsh reality of the state of your relationships with those around you, you are faced with a choice—to take action or to remain passive.

After identifying the gaps in relationships with the Gunas Scale, one has to work on filling those gaps. This is the action required to nurture EI/EQ. But why would people refrain from taking any action even when they've identified what they have to do? It boils down to the relationship between will and ability.

From Powerlessness to Possibility

Thomas Edison, one of history's greatest inventors, faced many failures while trying to create the lightbulb. He tried over a thousand times but kept failing. Instead of giving up, he chose not to feel powerless. When asked about his failures, Edison famously said, "I haven't failed. I've just found 10,000 ways that don't work."

Edison's persistence and positive attitude turned his failures into learning experiences, which eventually led to his success. His story shows that no matter how tough things seem, we can overcome obstacles if we stay determined and believe that each challenge brings us closer to success.

Like Edison, we all face failure and doubt, but his journey teaches us that by changing our mindset and not giving up, we can turn feelings of powerlessness into new possibilities and opportunities for success

The Unshakable Trust of Childhood

In a small village, two young boys, Rohan and Aryan, were the best of friends. One school holiday, they went out to play football in the fields. As they played, their laughter filled the air, and they unknowingly wandered deep into the nearby jungle, caught up in the fun.

Suddenly, Rohan slipped and disappeared from Aryan's view. Worried, Aryan rushed to find him and saw that Rohan had fallen into an old, dry well hidden under leaves. The well was deep, and Rohan's cries for help were faint.

Despite being scared, Aryan stayed calm and focused on helping his friend. Rohan noticed an old rope in the well and told Aryan to tie it around him and pull him up. Without hesitation, Aryan followed Rohan's instructions.

Using all his strength and with complete trust in himself, Aryan began to pull. To his surprise, Rohan started to rise. Aryan's determination, fueled by the trust he had in his friend and his belief in himself, allowed him to lift Rohan out of the well.

When they got home, their parents found it hard to believe the story. How could a young boy like Aryan pull his friend out of a deep well? But a wise elder in the village understood. He explained, "Aryan's strength wasn't just physical. It came from the trust and belief he had in himself. His parents had always encouraged him, and that gave him the confidence to face any challenge."

The elder added, "When we believe in ourselves, we can overcome even the hardest challenges. But when we doubt ourselves, even simple tasks can seem impossible."

This story of Rohan and Aryan shows how trust, belief, and determination can help us face difficulties and grow stronger.

The Role of EQ in Everyday Life

Emotional Quotient (EQ) is different from other types of intelligence because it focuses on understanding and using emotions. According to experts Mayer and Salovey, EQ is about recognizing our own feelings and those of others, and then using that emotional understanding to solve problems and manage our actions.

One key part of EQ is how it helps us act. What motivates us to work toward our goals? How does our determination impact our success? It's our ability to understand, control, and use our emotions that guides us in reaching our goals and making better decisions.

In simple terms, emotional quotient is what helps us stay calm under pressure, understand others better, and stay focused on what we want to achieve.

Achieving goals, whether personal or organisational, builds on two critical factors: will and ability. Both are essential, and their interconnection determines success.

1.High Will, High Ability:

Ideal for leadership and key roles, driving projects forward with both passion and skill.

2.High Will, Low Ability:

These individuals are eager to learn and grow, benefiting from training and mentorship to enhance their contributions.

3.Low Will, High Ability:

Skilled but unmotivated members can be re-engaged with the right incentives and alignment with their interests.

4.Low Will, Low Ability:

Require significant support and development; understanding their issues can lead to better role alignment or reassignment.

> **Will and Ability are indispensable for achieving success. Cultivating both within a team or individual maximizes potential and drives meaningful progress towards goals.**
>
> *-Rajeev Kharyal*

> **If you have a choice, choose the best but if you have no choice, do the best.**
>
> *-Prikshit Jobanputra*

The Inspiring Journey of Sheetal Devi

At 12 years old, Sheetal Devi, from a small village in Jammu and Kashmir, was facing the unique challenges of growing up with a rare condition called phocomelia, which left her with undeveloped upper limbs. Her life changed dramatically in 2019 when she attended a youth event where the Indian Army's Rashtriya Rifles unit recognized her confidence and potential. They supported her education and provided her with medical help. Soon after, army coaches Abhilasha Chaudhary and Kuldeep Wadhwan began training her in archery.

Although prosthetics were considered, it wasn't a viable option for Sheetal. Instead, she amazed her coaches with her ability to climb trees using only her legs. Inspired by armless archer Matt Stutzman, her coaches created a special training plan for her. Within 11 months of intense training, Sheetal's hard work paid off as she competed in the 2022 Asian Para Games, winning two gold medals and a silver medal in archery.

In 2023, Sheetal's achievements were recognized with the prestigious Arjuna Award, presented to her by the President of India in January 2024. Her journey, from a small village to becoming a world-class para-archer, shows that with strong willpower, support, and determination, even the most difficult challenges can be overcome.

Sheetal's story is a powerful reminder that no matter the obstacles, perseverance and belief in oneself can lead to extraordinary success. With the right mindset and support, limitations can be transformed into achievements.

The Importance of Intent in Reaching Goals

No matter where we are in life, the intent behind our actions plays a crucial role in shaping the results we achieve. While circumstances and privileges affect us, it is our purpose and intentions that truly guide us toward success or failure.

Intent is like an invisible force that drives our actions. When we act with positive intent—showing kindness, compassion, and honesty—it leads to better, more fulfilling outcomes. On the other hand, actions driven by selfishness or negativity often distance us from happiness and success.

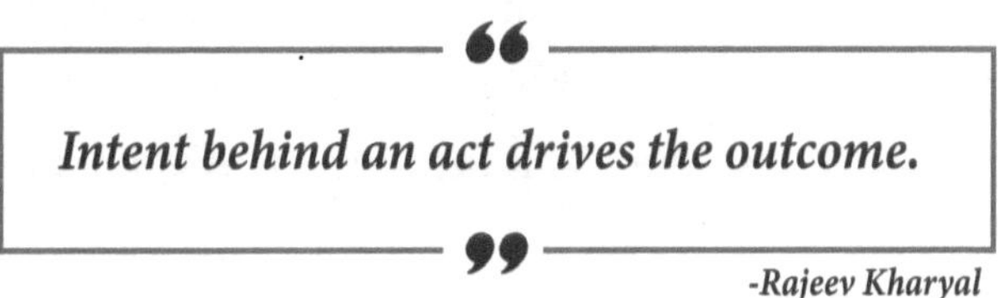

Intent behind an act drives the outcome.

-Rajeev Kharyal

When our actions are motivated by clear, positive intent, they can create powerful change, both for ourselves and others.

Example of Intent in Action: Rani Lakshmibai

A great example of how intent can shape outcomes is the story of Rani Lakshmibai, the Queen of Jhansi. In the mid-19th century, when India was under British rule, Lakshmibai was determined to protect her kingdom from British takeover. Even after the British refused to recognize her adopted son as the rightful heir, she didn't give up.

With a strong intent to defend her people and her kingdom, Rani Lakshmibai prepared for battle, training an army that included both men and women. Her leadership and bravery in fighting against the British became a symbol of resistance and inspired many others in the Indian rebellion of 1857.

Her famous words, **"I will not surrender my Jhansi,"** show her clear intent and determination. Even though she lost her life in battle, her legacy lives on as a symbol of courage and strength. Her story proves that when intent and action are aligned, even the toughest challenges can be faced with confidence.

The key to achieving personal growth and strong relationships is aligning our actions with positive intent. Every action, guided by clear purpose and values, contributes to our success and happiness. It's the conscious choice to act with good intent that leads us forward on the path to a fulfilling and enriching life

The Inspiring Story of Poorna Malavath

Poorna Malavath, at just 13 years old, became the youngest girl to climb Mount Everest. Her journey is a powerful example of how aligning intent with action can lead to amazing success. Growing up in a small tribal village in Telangana, India, Poorna's dream of climbing Everest seemed almost impossible due to her background and the physical challenges of such a feat. But her determination to break barriers and prove that "girls can do anything" kept her focused.

With the right support, intense training, and unwavering determination, Poorna turned her intent into action. She didn't just climb Everest to achieve a personal goal but to inspire other girls from marginalized communities to chase their dreams, no matter the obstacles.

Every step she took toward the top of the world's highest peak was a result of her clear purpose and intent. Poorna's story shows us how important it is to align our actions with clear & positive intent.

Her success came from perseverance, emotional strength, and a clear focus on her goal. This lesson applies to all of us—whether we are pursuing personal dreams or working toward organizational success. When we manage our emotions, stay focused, and match our actions to our purpose, we can achieve extraordinary things.

Emotional intelligence, unlike IQ, is something we can improve with time and practice. By acting with positive intent, as Poorna did, we open the door to personal growth and incredible achievements.

The Relentless Pursuit of Excellence

Sachin Tendulkar, a name recognized in nearly every Indian household, is celebrated for his outstanding cricket career. Known for his extraordinary batting skills, Sachin's career spanned over two decades, during which he set records that still inspire players today. He holds the record for the most runs in international cricket and has achieved an incredible 100 international centuries.

What made Sachin special wasn't just his records but his constant drive to improve. Whether scoring his first century at 17 or performing on the biggest stages, his focus was always on the ball and the game at hand. His career represents a relentless pursuit of excellence, leaving behind a legacy that goes beyond cricket.

This idea of constant improvement and striving for excellence connects to emotional intelligence as well. When we work on building emotional intelligence, we start a journey of self-growth. We become more aware of our own feelings, understand others better, and build stronger relationships. This self-awareness helps us make better choices in both our personal and professional lives.

Whether you are facing personal challenges or pursuing big goals, combining willpower, ability, and purposeful action unlocks incredible potential.

Chapter 9

Separate from the Herd

Ralph Waldo Emerson once said,

> **To be yourself in a world that is constantly trying to make you something else is the greatest accomplishment.**

This idea is vividly illustrated in the story of Naresh, a man walking through his village with a goat on his shoulder.

As Naresh walked, several people stopped him, insisting that the goat he was carrying was, in fact, a dog. At first, Naresh confidently corrected them, saying, "It's a goat, not a dog." However, as more people repeated this false claim, Naresh began to doubt his own senses. By the time a fourth person told him the same, he surrendered to the pressure, set the goat down, and walked away, convinced he had been wrong. The tricksters, who had conspired to confuse him, then stole the goat.

This story illustrates the powerful influence of others' opinions, even when we know the truth. When enough people around us repeat a falsehood, we start to question our own judgment, just as Naresh did. This phenomenon is known as herd mentality—the tendency to follow the crowd rather than trust our own beliefs. Breaking free from this mindset is essential for staying true to ourselves, especially in a world that constantly pressures us to conform. Believing in our understanding and values is one of the greatest strengths we can develop.

Freedom from Herd Mentality

Breaking free from herd mentality requires the courage to think independently, trust your beliefs, and avoid simply following the crowd. This process begins with self-awareness, enabling you to discover your true self. As you cultivate your individuality, you take control of your thoughts, actions, associations, and the information you choose to engage with. This empowers you to live with purpose, unlike those who, by blindly following others, lose their capacity for independent thought.

For those who embrace their uniqueness and trust their own judgments, the journey can be profoundly rewarding. They rise above societal pressures, unlocking their full potential. In contrast, those who remain trapped in herd mentality miss the opportunity to explore their creativity and true abilities. Once you understand your values, new paths open up—paths that not only benefit you but can also positively impact society.

Consider Galileo Galilei, a prominent example of breaking away from herd mentality. In the 17th century, most people, including the Church, believed that Earth was the center of the universe. Yet, Galileo's observations led him to conclude that Earth and the planets revolved around the Sun. Although challenging this belief was dangerous, Galileo trusted his discoveries. Despite persecution, he stood by the truth and revolutionized science.

Galileo's story teaches us that breaking free from herd mentality is challenging but crucial for personal growth and societal progress. Independent thinkers challenge the status quo, offering ideas that advance human understanding.

The Importance of Thinking for Yourself

A modern example of independent thinking comes from Yashwant Sinha, India's Finance Minister during Atal Bihari Vajpayee's administration. Since colonial times, India's Union Budget had been presented in the evening to align with the London Stock Exchange's working hours. For decades, no one questioned this practice—a clear example of herd mentality.

In 1999, the Hon'ble Prime Minister decided to break away from this outdated custom by presenting the budget in the morning, signaling that India's financial policies should serve its people, not be dictated by foreign traditions. This bold move not only ended a colonial-era practice but also showcased India's growing confidence in its own economic leadership.

This decision exemplifies how independent thinking in leadership can lead to practical, forward-thinking reforms. By refusing to adhere to "the way it's always been done," true leaders assess what is genuinely best for their people. This approach reminds us that challenging herd mentality can lead to meaningful progress.

Emotional Intelligence: The Key to True Leadership

To break free from herd mentality and avoid transactional leadership, emotional intelligence (EQ) is essential. EQ goes beyond understanding emotions; it involves using that understanding to build meaningful relationships, make thoughtful decisions, and navigate challenges with empathy and composure.

Leaders with high EQ manage stress effectively, make sound decisions under pressure, and inspire those around them with emotional stability. Self-awareness—a critical aspect of EQ—helps leaders recognize their strengths and weaknesses, aligning their choices with their core values. Developing EQ benefits leaders personally and creates environments where both individuals and organizations can thrive.

Galileo's courage to stand by his discoveries and Sinha's bold decision to challenge tradition are examples of emotionally intelligent leadership. Both individuals trusted their judgments and acted with conviction, even when facing opposition. Emotional intelligence allows leaders to rise above societal pressures, introducing fresh perspectives that drive progress.

The Temptation of Personal Profiteering

Often, individuals who understand and influence human psychology may succumb to personal profiteering, using their capabilities for self-gain or advancing agendas misaligned with the greater good.

Consider Elizabeth Holmes, founder of Theranos. Initially celebrated as a visionary, Holmes claimed her company had developed groundbreaking blood-testing technology. On the surface, she embodied innovation and emotional insight, positioning herself as a disruptor in healthcare. However, as investigations revealed, the technology was ineffective, and her company had misled investors, doctors, and patients. Holmes, once lauded as a genius, promoted a false narrative, putting public health at risk.

Her actions illustrate how individuals, armed with a keen understanding of human psychology, can exploit it for personal gain at the expense of societal well-being. *It serves as a reminder that without ethical grounding and a focus on the greater good, both IQ and EQ can be misused in ways ultimately detrimental to society.*

The Middlemen and Their Impact

The following cases highlight how middlemen across finance, healthcare, and corporate sectors can shape public perception and trust, emphasizing the importance of ethics, transparency, and accountability to prevent major crises:

1. Enron Corporation

Enron rapidly expanded in the 1990s, but behind the scenes, it used complex accounting tricks to hide massive debts and inflate profits.

Middlemen's Role: Accountants and financial analysts helped maintain Enron's illusion of success, misleading investors.

Outcome: When exposed in 2001, Enron's bankruptcy led to massive job losses and sparked regulations on corporate transparency, including the Sarbanes-Oxley Act.

2. 2008 Financial Crisis

The crisis was fueled by risky subprime mortgages and misleading financial products, triggering a global recession.

Middlemen's Role: Mortgage brokers issued risky loans, banks sold them as safe investments, and rating agencies endorsed them, masking true risks. The crisis underscored the dangers of unchecked financial practices and the importance of transparency.

3. Lehman Brothers

Lehman's aggressive investments in mortgage-backed securities made it vulnerable to market collapse, leading to bankruptcy.

Middlemen's Role: Advisors promoted high-risk investments, and rating agencies endorsed Lehman, fueling investor confidence. Lehman's collapse intensified the financial crisis, prompting regulatory changes.

4. Opioid Crisis

Pharmaceutical companies promoted opioids as safe, leading to widespread addiction and overdose deaths.

Middlemen's Role: Medical journals, sales reps, and healthcare providers promoted opioids based on company claims, ignoring addiction risks. The opioid crisis has led to severe health impacts and legal action, underscoring the need for ethical practices in healthcare marketing.

The Pursuit of Individuality

The risk in embracing individuality lies in disconnecting from ethical principles and a genuine desire to serve the greater good. When personal ambition turns solely toward self-fulfillment or power, it leads to emptiness. These individuals may become absorbed in a sense of superiority that fosters apathy and hedonistic tendencies.

For example, Anderson Silva, once regarded as one of the greatest fighters in mixed martial arts, tarnished his reputation by testing positive for steroids. Despite his achievements, this choice reflected a lapse in ethical grounding, turning what could have been an enduring legacy into a reminder of the dangers of unchecked ambition.

The Intangible Results of EQ

The lasting impact of EQ may be subtle but profound. Emotional intelligence fosters environments where personal and collective growth thrives, creating leaders who inspire and uplift those around them.

Chapter 10

Beyond the Horizon of the 13 Segment

> *We make a living by what we get,*
> *but we make a life by what we give.*
>
> *-Winston Churchill*

As people in the 13 segment become more self-aware and develop a strong sense of individuality, they have the power to use their skills and knowledge for many purposes. Unfortunately, as discussed in the previous chapter, some choose to use their understanding of human psychology for personal gain. These individuals may manipulate and control others to serve their own interests, focusing on profits rather than helping society.

Even though they may achieve wealth or influence, these individuals remain trapped in the limitations and ideas set by society. They may seem successful, but their actions are driven by self-interest rather than a greater purpose.

True success comes not just from what we get, but from what we give. When we use our knowledge and abilities to help others and make a positive impact, we move beyond the narrow mindset of personal gain and find greater fulfillment.

The Higher Calling of Awareness

Within the 13 segment, there is a group of people who don't become trapped by feelings of superiority or selfish goals. Instead, they are driven by a deeper understanding: that their awareness and knowledge are meant not for personal gain, but also for serving and improving society. They realize that true success comes from helping others, not just acquiring wealth or status.

These individuals understand that all beings are connected, and their actions have a larger impact on the world around them. They are guided by a higher purpose, using their emotional intelligence and skills to create positive change and lift others up.

A great example of this is Dr. A.P.J. Abdul Kalam. Coming from a humble background, he rose to become the Project Director of India's first Satellite Launch Vehicle (SLV-III). His journey shows his dedication to personal growth, hard work, and innovation. But what truly made him stand out was his focus on serving his country and improving society. His contributions to India's technological progress were not just about personal success—they were about uplifting the nation and making a lasting impact

Transcending the Materialistic Mindset

True growth in the 13 segment is achieved when individuals use their knowledge and skills for the greater good, rather than just for personal gain. Those who can rise above a materialistic mindset focus on helping society by using their emotional intelligence to benefit others. This shift from personal success to social contribution is the transition from Emotional Quotient (EQ) to Social Quotient (SQ).

A fitting example is the life of Emily Dickinson, an American poet who spent most of her life in isolation. While her emotional intelligence shines through in the depth of her poetry, her reclusiveness meant that her work had little impact during her lifetime. Most of her poetry was not published or recognized until after her death.

Dickinson's story reminds us that while developing personal talent is important, sharing that talent with others through social engagement can greatly amplify its impact. Cultivating both EQ and SQ allows us to use our abilities not just for ourselves but for the benefit of society

Leadership and Communal Responsibility

Some people on their journey of growth understand their responsibility to society and choose to work selflessly for the greater good. They use their leadership and people skills to inspire others, creating a ripple effect that promotes collective well-being.

A great example is E. Sreedharan, known as the "Metro Man of India." His leadership and dedication transformed public transportation in India, especially through his work on the Konkan Railway and the Delhi Metro—projects once thought impossible.

Sreedharan, born in 1932, pursued Civil Engineering and later earned a Master's degree in Structural Engineering. His career took off when he led the construction of the Kolkata Metro, laying the foundation for modern urban development in India. Later, he tackled the challenging 760-kilometer Konkan Railway project, which involved building bridges and tunnels through difficult terrain. His innovative leadership turned this complex task into a great success.

Sreedharan's most significant achievement is the Delhi Metro, which revolutionized public transport in the capital. His leadership, grounded in social responsibility, helped create something that benefited millions of people, making a lasting impact on India's urban infrastructure.

His story is an example of how true leaders use their skills not for personal gain but for the good of society. Sreedharan's contributions have earned him numerous awards, but more importantly, his work has changed the lives of many.

Key Takeaway: Leaders like Sreedharan show us that true success comes from using our skills and emotional intelligence to improve the world around us. By focusing on communal responsibility, they make a lasting impact, uniting communities and promoting progress for all

<h1 style="text-align:center">Section-B
Summary
(Chapters 6-10)</h1>

This section dives deeper into how society is divided and controlled, with a focus on awareness and self-growth. The framework of '3', '13', and '84' continues to guide the discussion, helping us understand how people in these groups experience and challenge societal structures.

The Role of the '13': The '13' segment represents individuals with heightened awareness and critical thinking. They question societal norms and often act as intermediaries between the unaware '84' and the powerful '3'. Their ability to understand people and situations helps them challenge dominant ideas and promote personal growth.

The Journey of Awareness: A key theme is the personal journey of the '13', which includes both intellectual and emotional development. This involves confronting uncomfortable truths about oneself and society, encouraging self-reflection and learning. This awareness helps individuals break free from societal conditioning and connect more deeply with their true selves and the world.

Emotional Quotient (EQ): The section explains how EQ helps the '13' better understand themselves and others. It serves as a tool for moving away from the herd mentality and societal pressure, showing how emotional intelligence empowers individuals to challenge limiting beliefs.

Social Programming and Its Impact: The narrative discusses how societal programming shapes thoughts and behaviors through cultural norms and institutions. It encourages readers to recognize and question these ingrained beliefs to embrace new perspectives and think critically.

The Downfall of the '13': Some individuals in the '13' segment misuse their awareness for personal gain, which leads to their downfall. By focusing only on self-interest, they lose sight of long-term success and personal growth.

Manipulation and Control: The section highlights how some people in the '13' segment use their knowledge to manipulate information, control resources, and divide people for personal benefit. Recognizing these tactics helps individuals break free from this control and think more independently.

Awareness for Personal Profiteering: Finally, the chapters explore how some in the '13' use their social and emotional awareness not to help others, but for personal profit. They craft stories that influence the masses for their own advantage, rather than promoting collective well-being.

> *Key Takeaway: These chapters encourage readers to develop self-awareness and emotional intelligence, while warning against the misuse of knowledge for selfish purposes*

The Altruistic Path

Introduction: Emotional and Altruism

True greatness lies not just in achieving personal success but in using that success to uplift others. This is where Emotional Quotient (EQ)—the ability to understand and manage emotions—comes into play. EQ helps us grow as individuals, but its highest value is found when we use it to serve others and create a positive impact.

How do you use your emotional intelligence? Do you focus on personal growth, or do you also apply it to support those around you?

Leaders who recognize that EQ can drive positive change can make a lasting impact. This is where Social Quotient (SQ) comes in—the ability to take personal understanding and transform it into meaningful contributions to society.

The Origins of Social Quotient (SQ)

The idea of Social Quotient (SQ) was first introduced in 1920 by psychologist Edward Thorndike, who described it as

> **66**
>
> *The ability to understand and manage people*
> *and to act wisely in human relationships.*
>
> **99**

Over time, it became clearer that SQ plays a crucial role in both personal and professional success.

What do you think is more important—EQ or SQ? Or is it the combination of both that leads to greater success?

Today, it's obvious that how we connect with others influences our success. SQ helps us understand others' emotions and navigate relationships effectively. Howard Gardner expanded on this idea with his concept of "interpersonal intelligence," which closely aligns with Daniel Goleman's work on EQ.

Social Intelligence in Action

Daniel Goleman's book, *Social Intelligence: The New Science of Human Relationships,* explains that social intelligence is made up of two main components: social awareness (understanding others) and relationship management (working well with others). Combined with EQ, these skills form Emotional and Social Intelligence (ESI).

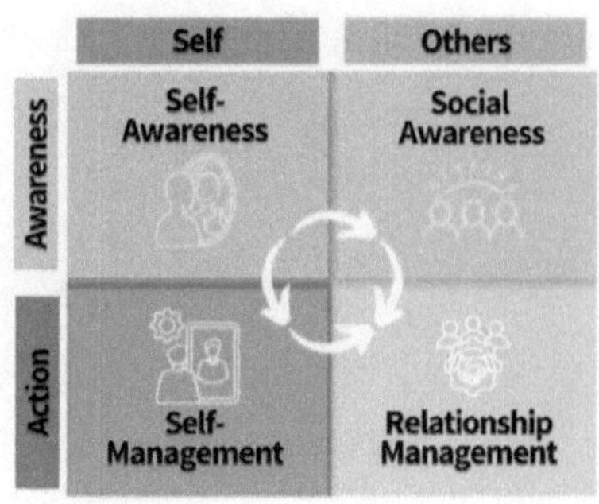

Leaders with high ESI stand out because they don't just use these skills for their own benefit—they use them to make a difference in the lives of others.

Real-World Examples of Social Quotient (SQ)

Azim Premji, the chairman of Wipro, is a perfect example of someone who uses SQ not only for business success but for social good. Through the Azim Premji Foundation, he works to improve education in rural India, helping teachers and providing resources to underprivileged children. Premji's ability to connect his personal success with social responsibility is a powerful demonstration of how SQ can be used to transform lives.

Another great example is Aruna Roy, a social activist who played a key role in creating India's Right to Information (RTI) Act. Roy's SQ allowed her to understand the needs of rural communities and organize people to demand transparency from the government. Her ability to connect with people and rally them for a cause shows how SQ can drive real social change.

Who are the leaders or activists you admire? How do they use social intelligence in their work?

Understanding Social Quotient (SQ)

Think of Social Quotient (SQ) as a skill that develops over time, as we engage with others and learn from social experiences. We are naturally social creatures, and our ability to navigate complex relationships shapes much of our personal and professional success.

Here's a helpful way to understand the difference between social awareness and SQ:

- **Social awareness** is like being a skilled player on a cricket team: you know the game, understand your teammates, and can read your opponents—just like understanding the emotions and behaviors of those around you.

- **Social quotient** is like being the coach: not only do you understand the game, but you can also strategize and lead the team toward success—similar to how you use your understanding of people to create positive outcomes.

In simple terms, social awareness helps you understand others, while SQ allows you to use that understanding to make a difference.

Developing Social Intelligence Over Time

Social intelligence, like EQ, is a skill that evolves with time and experience. While most of us understand basic social interactions, handling more complex social situations requires constant refinement. Social intelligence isn't an automatic trait—it's something that needs practice and effort to develop.

From an early age, we start learning how to interpret social cues. Research shows that babies begin recognizing social signals by six weeks old, and by 18 months, they can understand more complex social behaviors. As we grow, our social environments become more intricate, and we must continue to sharpen our social skills to navigate these changing dynamics.

Field Marshal Sam Manekshaw:
A Leader with High Social Quotient (SQ)

Field Marshal Sam Manekshaw's high social quotient (SQ) was one of his defining qualities as a leader, setting him apart not only in military strategy but also in his skillful management of relationships and ethical decision-making. His SQ enabled him to navigate complex interpersonal dynamics, both within the military and with political leaders, in ways that ultimately contributed to the successful liberation of Bangladesh in 1971.

Relationship-Building with Political Leaders: Manekshaw's ability to build trusting relationships with political leaders showcased his high SQ. Known for his forthrightness and unshakable ethical standards, he was never afraid to voice his strategic opinions, even when they contradicted political pressures. His interactions with then-Prime Minister Indira Gandhi, for instance, were marked by mutual respect and clear communication. Rather than bending to immediate political demands to take action against Pakistan, he diplomatically explained the importance of waiting for the right moment, prioritizing the well-being of his troops and the mission's long-term success. This nuanced handling of his relationship with political authorities enabled him to make sound decisions without compromising his principles or alienating key stakeholders.

Empathy and Connection with Soldiers: Manekshaw's empathy toward his soldiers was another testament to his high SQ. He understood the importance of morale and how deeply a leader's behavior impacts those under their command. Known for his down-to-earth personality, he

often mingled with troops, addressing their concerns, sharing light-hearted moments, and providing reassurances during challenging times. This approach fostered a strong sense of trust and loyalty, as soldiers felt respected and valued. His ability to connect with his troops on a personal level demonstrated his understanding of social dynamics, which proved essential in maintaining unity and morale throughout the 1971 war.

Legacy of Social Quotient in Leadership: Manekshaw's legacy exemplifies how high SQ can profoundly impact both immediate team dynamics and broader societal outcomes. His ability to manage relationships, connect with others, and uphold ethical standards earned him respect not only from his peers but also from subsequent generations. His life teaches that a leader's success is greatly influenced by their social intelligence—the capacity to build trust, navigate complex relationships, and maintain moral integrity, even in the face of adversity. This legacy underscores the lasting value of SQ in effective, compassionate leadership

Chapter 12

The Journey of Lasting Impact

Throughout our careers, there comes a moment when we realize that success isn't measured solely by personal achievements but by the difference we make in the world around us. For me, this turning point came in 2002, during the privatization and restructuring of Delhi's power sector. The changes happening around me presented a challenge but also an opportunity to do something more—to drive meaningful change not just for myself but for the community I served.

As district manager at BSES Rajdhani Power Limited, I faced the responsibility of not only navigating this complex shift but also of ensuring that my actions had a lasting, positive impact. In this transformative phase, I began to see how the key to solving complex issues lay not in overly technical jargon, but in simplifying the message. This was when I fully grasped the power of *Albert Einstein's words:*

> **If you can't explain it simply,
> you don't understand it well enough.**

Simplifying Complexity: Power Distribution and Human Connection

In my role, I often developed analogies to bridge the gap between technical complexity and human understanding. One of the most impactful analogies I used compared the human body to a power system. This metaphor made it easier for stakeholders to understand how low, high, and extra-high voltage systems function. By linking voltage levels to how our body operates, I simplified a complex system, allowing people to grasp the bigger picture more easily.

Just as electricity flows through transmission lines and steps down through transformers before reaching homes, the human body functions in a similar layered system. The upper body manages vital functions, the middle body supports essential processes, and the lower body handles smaller, routine tasks. Each part plays a critical role in maintaining balance, much like different voltage levels in power distribution—where every stage is necessary for the system to work smoothly.

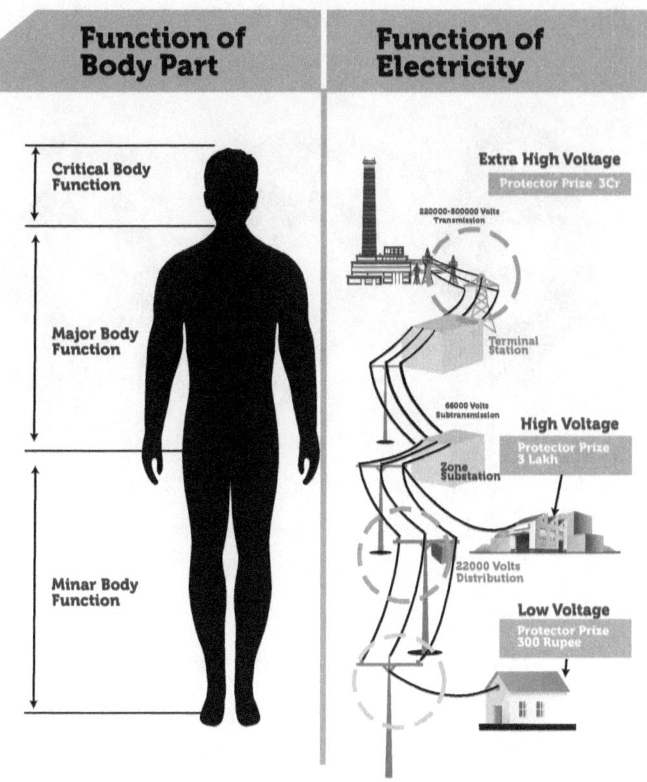

This analogy didn't just clarify technical aspects of power transmission; it also helped people from different departments collaborate more effectively. It fostered a shared understanding, highlighting that breaking down silos and working together is key to innovation. Collaboration, much like efficient power distribution, requires every layer to communicate and function in harmony.

At a deeper level, this analogy also illustrates a profound connection between power and life itself. Just as electricity is invisible but essential as it flows through conductors, the soul is invisible yet vital as it animates the body, and blood flows through veins like current through wires. Both systems, though unseen, are fundamental to sustaining life—whether it's the life of a city powered by electricity or the life of a body energized by the flow of blood. This invisible yet powerful connection underscores how essential these forces are, even when we cannot see them.

Gandhi's Timeless Wisdom: Applying the Five Senses to Leadership

Mahatma Gandhi Ji's profound message, "Think twice before you speak" and "See no evil, hear no evil, speak no evil," resonated deeply with me during this time. His teachings about the mindful use of our senses inspired me to explore new analogies, and I began to see how the five senses, like the layers of a power system, are essential to effective leadership.

In a world that often values speaking over listening, Gandhi Ji's teachings reminded me of the immense power of silence and reflection. The tongue, unlike sight or hearing, has no backup—what we say cannot be unsaid. This realization reinforced for me the critical importance of thoughtful communication in leadership, where every word can have lasting impact. Just as different voltages in a power system must be carefully managed to prevent damage, the way we manage our communication can prevent misunderstandings and foster clarity.

Furthermore, just as protective equipment becomes more advanced with higher voltage to safeguard critical parts, the human body has evolved complex systems to protect its most vital functions. In leadership, I compared the five senses to 'extra-high voltage,' emphasizing their significance. Our senses—what we see, hear, and say—are our key inputs in decision-making, and safeguarding them is essential. This analogy helped stakeholders understand why it's so important to optimize and protect these sensory inputs for clear and effective leadership.

By drawing these parallels, I was able to simplify the importance of mindful communication, empathy, and clear decision-making—core aspects of leadership. Just as power distribution relies on efficient, invisible systems working together, leadership thrives when thoughtful communication and mindful awareness come together, ensuring clarity and progress

Seizing the Moment: "Strike While the Iron Is Hot"

This chapter of my career underscored one of the most important lessons I've learned: timing is everything. The old saying, "Strike while the iron is hot," became a guiding principle. Hot iron is malleable and easy to shape, just as life's opportunities are when seized at the right time. If you wait too long, the iron cools, and it becomes difficult—if not impossible—to shape it as intended.

In the power sector, as in life, it's not just about having the right tools, but knowing when and how to use them. Timing, agility, and the ability to recognize when the moment is right make all the difference in creating lasting change.

Social Quotient (SQ): Leading with Empathy and Awareness

As I reflect on these experiences, I've come to understand the true importance of Social Quotient (SQ). High SQ reflects a leader's ability to not only understand social dynamics but to navigate them with empathy and foresight. It's about more than individual success; it's about recognizing how interconnected we all are and ensuring that our actions benefit the people and communities around us.

People with high SQ understand that opportunities, like heated iron, are fleeting, and they act quickly but thoughtfully to make a lasting impact. High SQ is what turns ordinary leadership into transformative leadership.

Raman, the "Riverman of India,"

has steadfastly worked towards improving small rivers, water quality, and availability despite social, personal, and financial challenges. When the Double Village community faced water problems, Raman selflessly funded water testing, demonstrating his commitment. His strong will has driven policymakers to establish a long-term drinking water system for the community. Raman's exceptional leadership and team management skills have shaped river policies in Western Uttar Pradesh, a complex task requiring adaptability. As a strong leader, Raman inspires shared vision and collective action. Articulate on rural and urban environmental issues, Raman shares expertise at local, national, and international seminars, advocating inclusive planning. Alongside his team, Raman continues contributing to societal well-being, embodying dedication and vision. Hon'ble President of India has well appreciated his contribution and passion.

Chetan Singh Solanki,

the "Solar Man of India," is a renowned professor of Energy Science at IIT Bombay and founder of the Energy Swaraj Foundation. His pioneering work in solar energy has transformed India's energy landscape. Solanki's contributions include developing affordable solar solutions, designing solar-powered irrigation systems, and improving solar cell efficiency. He has also implemented solar-powered electrification projects in rural India. He has advised government agencies on solar energy policy and contributed to India's National Solar Mission. As a prolific researcher, Solanki has authored numerous papers and edited books on solar energy and sustainability. His dedication has electrified rural communities, created livelihood opportunities, and promoted energy literacy. Through his work, Solanki embodies the spirit of sustainability and continues to inspire future generations.

Nagendra Singh,

An engineer from IIT BHU, founded ENF Coaching along with co founders with a vision to provide quality education to underprivileged students. The initiative focuses on supporting students from economically disadvantaged backgrounds who aspire to gain admission into premier engineering and medical colleges.

They partner with companies that allocate funds from their CSR budgets. This collaboration enables the initiative to offer quality education at no or nominal cost . This bridges the education gap between the privileged and underprivileged and foster a more inclusive and equitable society.

Seizing Opportunities: Lessons from Oprah and Morita

Few leaders embody high SQ as well as Oprah Winfrey. Her journey from poverty to becoming one of the most influential figures in media was a masterclass in recognizing the right moments to act. Winfrey's ability to leverage her empathy, resilience, and understanding of people allowed her to shape not only her career but the lives of millions. Her success is a testament to the power of striking while the iron is hot, and using that moment to uplift others.

Similarly, Akio Morita, co-founder of Sony, showed the value of SQ in business. Morita believed in learning from mistakes, adapting quickly, and seizing opportunities when they arose. His ability to combine technical knowledge (IQ), emotional understanding (EQ), and social awareness (SQ) helped Sony become a global leader in innovation.

SQ: The Key to Lasting Leadership

While IQ measures intelligence and EQ gauges emotional intelligence, SQ is what ties everything together. Leaders with high SQ recognize that their success is intertwined with the success of those around them. They understand that knowledge alone isn't enough—true leadership requires empathy, awareness, and the ability to act in the best interests of others.

Chapter 13

The Diverging Paths of 13 and 3

Mirror Neurons: The "Wi-Fi" of Empathy

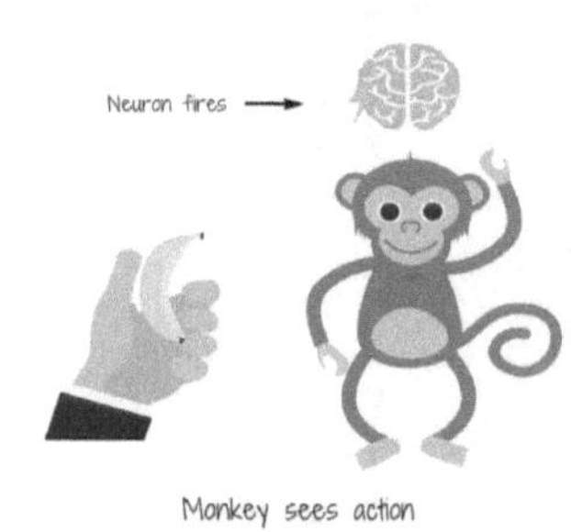

Recent discoveries in neuroscience reveal the power of mirror neurons, special brain cells that help us connect with others by reflecting their emotions and actions. Initially discovered in monkeys, these neurons fire both when we perform an action and when we observe someone else doing the same. This unique feature allows us to empathize with others, creating a bridge of emotional connection.

Mirror neurons act like "Wi-Fi" for the brain, syncing us with others and enabling us to share their experiences. For example, when we see someone laugh or cry, our brain reflects their emotions, allowing us to feel what they feel. This capacity for empathy, powered by mirror neurons, is a cornerstone of our Social Quotient (SQ)—our ability to connect with and care for others.

Empathy not only strengthens relationships but also shapes our worldview. It presents a choice: do we use this ability to foster connection and adopt a Mindset 3, or do we remain focused on ourselves, trapped in a Mindset 13?

Empathy in Action: Emotional Connection in Movies: A beautiful example of empathy can be found in the film Taare Zameen Par. The story revolves around Ishaan, a dyslexic boy whose art teacher helps him discover his potential. In a key moment, Ishaan wins an art competition, and his parents beam with pride.

Watching this scene, we feel Ishaan's triumph and his parents' joy as if it were our own. This emotional resonance is the result of mirror neurons firing in our brains, demonstrating the profound impact of empathy on human connection.

The Two Mindsets: Fear vs. Empathy

Mindset 13: Fear and Self-Interest

Driven by Scarcity: Believes resources are limited, leading to competition and hoarding, Prioritizes Personal Gain: Actions are often self-serving and disregard others' well-being, Historical Example: Alauddin Khilji expanded his empire through ruthless exploitation, prioritizing conquest over compassion, leaving behind mistrust and suffering.

Mindset 3: Empathy and Abundance

Driven by Compassion: Believes in shared growth and collective well-being, Prioritizes Connection: Happiness and success stem from collaboration and meaningful relationships, Historical Example: Vinoba Bhave's Bhoodan (Land Gift) movement inspired people to donate land for equitable distribution, fostering community and social harmony.

Our mirror neurons allow us to feel both fear and empathy. The mindset we choose—Mindset 13 or Mindset 3—determines the quality of our relationships, happiness, and societal impact.

Why People Get Stuck in Mindset 13

Despite the appeal of Mindset 3, many remain trapped in Mindset 13 due to barriers:

Internal Barriers: Lack of clarity in personal goals and purpose, Fear of leaving the comfort zone, Emotional baggage and limiting beliefs, Overemphasis on external validation over self-fulfilment.

External Barriers: Societal and cultural pressures that reward competition over collaboration, Social media comparisons fostering envy and dissatisfaction, Limited exposure to empathetic role models or supportive communities.

Consequences: Stagnation in personal and professional growth, Disconnection from core values and purpose, A life driven by short-term gains but devoid of long-term fulfilment.

Contrasting Mindsets: Social Media vs. Hotel Industry

Aspect	Mindset 13: Social Media Industry	Mindset 3: Hotel Industry
Priorities	Advertising revenue, user data collection.	Customer satisfaction, comfort, personalized care.
Actions	Exploiting data, amplifying sensational content.	Tailoring services, investing in staff development.
Consequences	Data breaches, misinformation, mental health impacts.	Loyal customers, positive reviews, repeat business.

This comparison illustrates how empathy-driven actions (Mindset 3) lead to sustainable success, while self-interest (Mindset 13) creates long-term challenges.

Applications Across Contexts

Healthcare

Mindset 3: Patient-centered care and public health advocacy.

Mindset 13: Focus on profits and prestige.

Engineering

Mindset 3: Sustainable, innovative solutions.

Mindset 13: Cost-cutting at the expense of long-term consequences.

Education

Mindset 3: Encourages critical thinking and adaptability.

Mindset 13: Prioritizes test scores and personal accolades.

Workplace Relationships

Mindset 3: Collaboration, trust, and shared goals.

Mindset 13: Competition, isolation, and inefficiency.

Financial Success and Happiness: Mindset 13 vs. Mindset 3

Mindset 13: Focuses on wealth and status, often sacrificing long-term well-being.

Mindset 3: Balances personal growth with societal impact, measuring success through relationships, fulfillment, and legacy.

Question: Can a person struggling with addictions like alcohol, drugs, or sexual impurity still be part of the Top 3% League?

Answer: Initially, they might have been part of the Top 3% League, but once trapped in these self-destructive habits, they'll inevitably slide down, much like a player who lands on a snake in the game of Snakes and Ladders. To regain their spot in the Top 3% League, they must overcome these addictions and develop healthier habits.

The distinguishing characteristic between the 13% and the 3% is the alignment of their thoughts, words, and actions. This congruence is the yardstick that measures a person's integrity and authenticity.

Key Statistics Supporting Mindset 3:

Purpose at Work: 85% of employees feel motivated when working toward a meaningful mission (Gallup).

Employee Retention: Organizations with purpose see 2.6x higher retention (Glassdoor).

Mental Health: 90% of volunteers report improved mental health (Corporation for National and Community Service).

Business Success: Companies prioritizing social responsibility outperform others by 2.5x (Harvard Business Review).

Taking Flight: Transitioning to Mindset 3

Transitioning from Mindset 13 to Mindset 3 is like breaking free from gravity and learning to soar. Selfish goals act like weights, anchoring us to narrow thinking and personal limitations. By shifting to selfless intentions, we free ourselves to rise toward greater meaning and purpose. Just as airplanes overcome the constraints of road travel to effortlessly cover vast distances, adopting Mindset 3 empowers us to transcend self-centeredness and embrace a higher, more fulfilling way of living

The Ripple Effect of Good Actions

Small acts of kindness can create ripples of change. Kailash Satyarthi, a social reformer, rescued thousands of children from labor exploitation, transforming lives and inspiring systemic change. This ripple effect reminds us that consistent, selfless actions can have far-reaching impacts

Rickshaw Ride: A Lesson in Service and Intent

One day, Mr. Kumar, a tired traveler, arrived at a train station and needed a ride to the bus terminal. He saw an elderly rickshaw puller and asked for a ride. "How much will it cost?" Mr. Kumar asked.

The rickshaw puller smiled and said, "I have three options: twenty rupees, forty rupees, or sixty rupees."

Surprised, Mr. Kumar asked, "Why the different prices?"

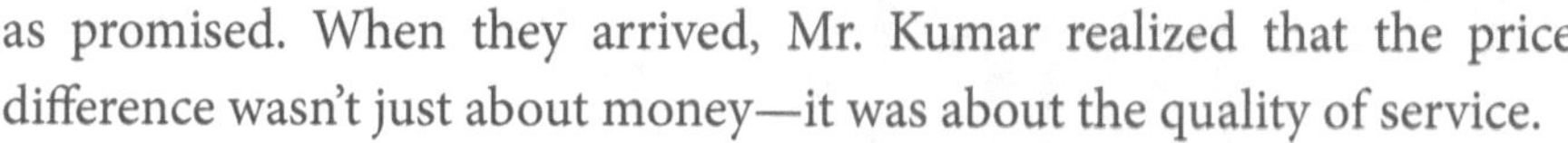

The rickshaw puller explained, "For twenty rupees, you can drive the rickshaw yourself. For forty rupees, I'll pull the rickshaw, but you'll feel every bump on the road. For sixty rupees, I'll pull the rickshaw and make sure the ride is smooth and comfortable."

Mr. Kumar chose the sixty-rupee option, and the rickshaw puller delivered a smooth, pleasant ride, as promised. When they arrived, Mr. Kumar realized that the price difference wasn't just about money—it was about the quality of service.

This story teaches us a valuable lesson about intent and service. People with the "13 mindset" might focus only on getting by with minimal effort, while those with the "3 mindset" put care into their actions and ensure the quality of the journey for themselves and others. The way we approach our actions shapes not only our experiences but the legacy we leave behind.

Conclusion: Choosing Empathy Over Fear

The journey between Mindset 13 and Mindset 3 is transformative. By embracing empathy and prioritizing connection over self-interest, we unlock deeper fulfillment, create meaningful relationships, and leave a lasting legacy.

What steps can you take today to shift toward a Mindset 3 approach and create ripples of positive change in the world?

Chapter 14

The Impact of the 3

Our actions and desires unite us as a community, often driving us to contribute positively. Whether it's building schools, cleaning neighborhoods, or supporting local businesses, these efforts stem from a shared commitment to improving the world around us.

Reflecting on my own journey, I realized early on that personal growth and helping society go hand in hand. Mentors and role models taught me an important lesson: *True progress happens when we focus not only on ourselves but also on the well-being of others.* This insight became the foundation for my passion to make a meaningful difference in my professional life.

The Singapore Experience and Nationalism

As we grow more aware of ourselves and our surroundings, we often feel a natural drive to make things better. Early in my career, I experienced this after visiting Singapore. Their advanced power system left a lasting impression on me, sparking a deep sense of nationalism, inspired by the teachings of Swami Vivekananda. This motivation fueled my desire to contribute to India's energy sector, even in the smallest way possible.

This drive led me to work in the reforms department of Delhi Vidyut Board, under the dynamic leadership of Shri SR Sethi. During a challenging transition period, a model district was created at Nehru Place, showcasing best practices in electricity distribution. It set a standard for private companies, helping to make the early stages of privatization smoother and more successful.

Creating Tangible Change

As Scottish philosopher Thomas Carlyle wisely said:

66

> *To reform a world, to reform a nation, no wise man will undertake; and all but foolish men know that the only solid, though far slower, reformation, is what each begins and perfects on himself.*

99

This understanding prompted me to shift my career focus in 2003. I moved away from personal gain to concentrate on improving customer service and delivery. I left a secure government job with unparalleled retirement benefits and took on a challenging role at Tata Power DDL. With the support of the charismatic leader Mr. Anil Sardana, then-CEO, I led the Key Customer Group during a time when I faced challenges that tested my persistence. This period also taught me the importance of enhancing my management skills, leading me to pursue further education at IIM Bangalore while continuing my work. On completion of this, I rose to leadership roles under the mentorship of Mr Ajai Narula, COO.

Addressing India's Electricity Challenges

In 2014, India faced a low global ranking in terms of access to electricity. As part of the "Make in India" initiative, there was a push to improve the country's standing in the World Bank's Ease of Doing Business (EoDB) index. At that time, it took over four months to get electricity—a major hurdle for businesses.

The dynamic leader and then-CEO, Mr. Praveer Sinha, appointed me to represent Tata Power DDL and fully supported me throughout the journey. Despite numerous challenges, our company worked tirelessly to find solutions. We presented proposals that convinced higher authorities and decision-makers. By 2020, our efforts paid off, as India's ranking for access to electricity improved from 137th to 22nd out of 190 countries. This was a significant achievement, reducing bureaucratic hurdles and improving infrastructure. India's overall EoDB ranking also jumped from 142nd to 63rd—a success widely appreciated by the Government of India.

During the above tenure, Dr Praveer Sinha became Tata Power CEO&MD and then Mr Sanjay Banga and later Mr Ganesh Srinivasan were CEO of our company. Senior Govt Officials who led this EoDB at DIPP were by Mr Amitabh Kant as Secretary, DIPP (who is presently India G 20 Sherpa), later Mr Ramesh Abhishek led this project along with Mr Shailendra Singh, Addl Secretary, DIPP along with many other senior officials. The policy reforms approvals wrt Power were primarily done under the Mr PK Sinha, Secretary (Power) who were later elevated to Cabinet Secretary. I was part of delegation led by four Secretaries of GoI went to World Bank, Washington DC office to represent mid course progress on project in 2017 which was very successful in the journey of EoDB ranking.

The True Meaning of Altruism

As I reflected on my journey, I realized that altruism isn't about seeking recognition; it's about making the world a better place without expecting anything in return. Altruism is about compassion and creating a positive impact in the community.

Often, altruism is viewed as overly idealistic, but in reality, it is a key aspect of social intelligence—the ability to see how we're all connected and to act in ways that benefit everyone. A perfect example of altruism is Dr. Gourav Aggarwal, an industrialist from Haryana. He once suffered from a severe skin disease that no treatment could cure until he turned to Ayurvedic medicine and healed himself through trial and error.

Not only did Dr. Aggarwal heal himself, but he also developed a medicine that cures gangrene, a condition affecting diabetic patients. For over a decade, he has treated hundreds of patients without seeking personal gain. I, too, benefited from his treatment when caught by this critical disease during the COVID-19 pandemic. His generosity and selflessness exemplify the essence of true altruism.

The Power of Personal Honesty

Personal honesty is crucial for building trust and integrity. Throughout my career, I faced moments where my honesty was tested. One notable instance occurred at Tata Power DDL during the rollout of a new technology. There were concerns that the technology might not work as expected, and I felt pressure to move forward despite the risks.

As the project leader, I chose transparency, explaining both the potential benefits and risks to all involved. This wasn't easy, but it led to a more thoughtful and collaborative approach. We conducted thorough tests before launching the technology on a large scale, which helped us identify key issues that needed to be addressed. Being honest not only prevented potential problems but also strengthened trust within the team.

"Urja Arpan" Initiative of TPDDL

At TPDDL, alongside enhancing services to improve customer experience in acquiring new connections, we have prioritized energy conservation and environmental sustainability. This commitment gave birth to the "Urja Arpan" initiative, aimed at promoting the adoption of energy-efficient appliances. Key initiatives included encouraging the use of LED bulbs instead of traditional incandescent bulbs, BLDC fans in place of conventional fans, electric vehicles (EVs), and solar energy solutions.

The significance of energy conservation becomes evident with compelling data: saving just 100 units of electricity prevents the emission of 79 kg of CO_2—equivalent to the annual oxygen production of three mature trees.

A cornerstone of the "Urja Arpan" initiative is the Behavioral Demand Response (BDR) program through participating customers voluntarily.

Urja Arpan initiative has been strongly supported by key partners such as the Bureau of Energy Efficiency (BEE), The Energy and Resources Institute (TERI), IIT Roorkee, and esteemed academic institutions like IIT Delhi, Faculty of Management Studies (FMS), and Shri Ram College of Commerce (SRCC). These institutions have significantly contributed to driving customer behavior changes towards adopting sustainable practices.

Visionary leaders, including Dr. Vibha Dhawan (Director General, TERI), Dr. Vivek Suneja (then Dean, FMS), Dean IIT Delhi Prof. Abhijit

Abhyankar , and Dr. Rhythm Singh (IIT Roorkee), have played pivotal roles in ensuring the success of "Urja Arpan," making it a visible and impactful initiative among stakeholders.

Building on the success of the Ease of Doing Business (EoDB) initiative, I had the honor of leading "Urja Arpan" under visionary leader, Mr. Ganesh Srinivasan (then CEO), and our dedicated team.

Sister Shivani, a renowned spiritual leader from the Brahma Kumaris blessed the initiative with a heartfelt speech, highlighting the deep connection between inner peace and a sustainable world.

Embracing Compassion and Purpose

As we grow, we realize that wealth and status are fleeting. True fulfillment comes from making a meaningful impact and helping others. The choice is simple: we can focus on ourselves and act out of fear, or we can embrace empathy and compassion to create a better world for everyone.

Altruism, personal honesty, and social intelligence are not just ideas— they are daily tools for making ethical decisions and creating a positive impact on those around us.

Chapter 15

The Hierarchy of IQ, EQ, and SQ: Bronze, Silver, and Gold

Achieving true excellence in life requires balancing three key elements: IQ, EQ, and SQ.

IQ (Intelligence Quotient) is about our ability to think critically, solve problems, and make smart decisions. It helps us navigate complex challenges and come up with effective solutions.

EQ (Emotional Quotient) is about understanding emotions—both our own and others'. It helps us build meaningful relationships, manage social interactions, and show empathy in everyday situations.

SQ (Social Quotient) focuses on social responsibility and leadership. It's the ability to work well within society, make ethical choices, and contribute to the greater good. People with high SQ think beyond themselves and aim to improve the world around them.

These three aspects—IQ, EQ, and SQ—work together to create a balanced approach to success and fulfilment in life.

The Hierarchy of IQ, EQ, and SQ: Bronze, Silver, and Gold

To make this triad easier to understand, we can compare IQ, EQ, and SQ to a bronze, silver, and gold hierarchy:

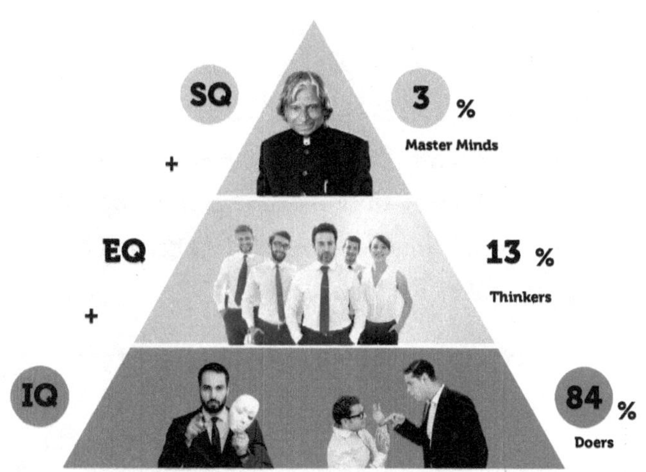

Bronze (IQ): The 84%

The Bronze level represents 84% of people who primarily rely on their intellectual abilities—thinking and problem-solving. These individuals work hard and have the basic skills needed for success. However, they tend to measure success by material achievements, status, or external validation. They often overlook the emotional and social dimensions of life, which can leave them feeling unfulfilled.

Silver (EQ): The 13%

The Silver level represents 13% of people who combine intelligence with emotional awareness. They are creative, flexible thinkers who excel not only in using their IQ but also in understanding and managing emotions. While they seek personal growth and deeper meaning, they are still on the path—navigating the challenges of societal expectations and finding their true purpose.

Gold (SQ): The 3%

The top 3% of people demonstrate mastery of both IQ and EQ, but their defining trait is their high Social Quotient (SQ). These individuals go beyond personal success. They use their intelligence and empathy to make a positive impact on the world, driven by a sense of responsibility and purpose. For them, success is not merely about personal gain, but about uplifting others and contributing to the greater good.

Beyond the Podium

> **66**
>
> *Just as gold, silver, and bronze represent the varying degree of effort, dedication, and focus in competitions, their value reflects the profound difference each achievement makes on the world.*
>
> **99**

-Rajeev Kharyal

SQ: The Peak of Leadership and Social Impact

While IQ and EQ are essential for personal success, SQ elevates individuals to the next level by focusing on the broader impact of their actions. People with high SQ exhibit ethical leadership and a strong sense of social responsibility. They don't just focus on their own success but strive to make a difference in the world.

An inspiring example of high SQ is Malala Yousafzai. Despite personal risks, she fought for girls' education in Pakistan. Her intelligence, emotional resilience, and commitment to social justice have positively impacted millions of lives, showing what it means to act for the greater good. This is what high SQ looks like—using influence to benefit others and creating lasting change.

The Journey from IQ to SQ: A Game of Snakes and Ladders

The journey from Bronze (IQ) to Silver (EQ) to Gold (SQ) can be compared to the game of snakes and ladders. While progress can be made, setbacks can also occur due to distractions or personal ambition. Staying on the path requires persistence and focus.

A historical example is Aurangzeb, the sixth Mughal emperor of India. He started with good intentions to improve governance, but over time, his focus shifted to expanding power and territory. He neglected his people's needs, leading to endless wars and social unrest. This story is a reminder that success without social responsibility (SQ) can lead to failure and discontent. True excellence requires keeping the greater good in mind at all times.

Snakes & Ladders

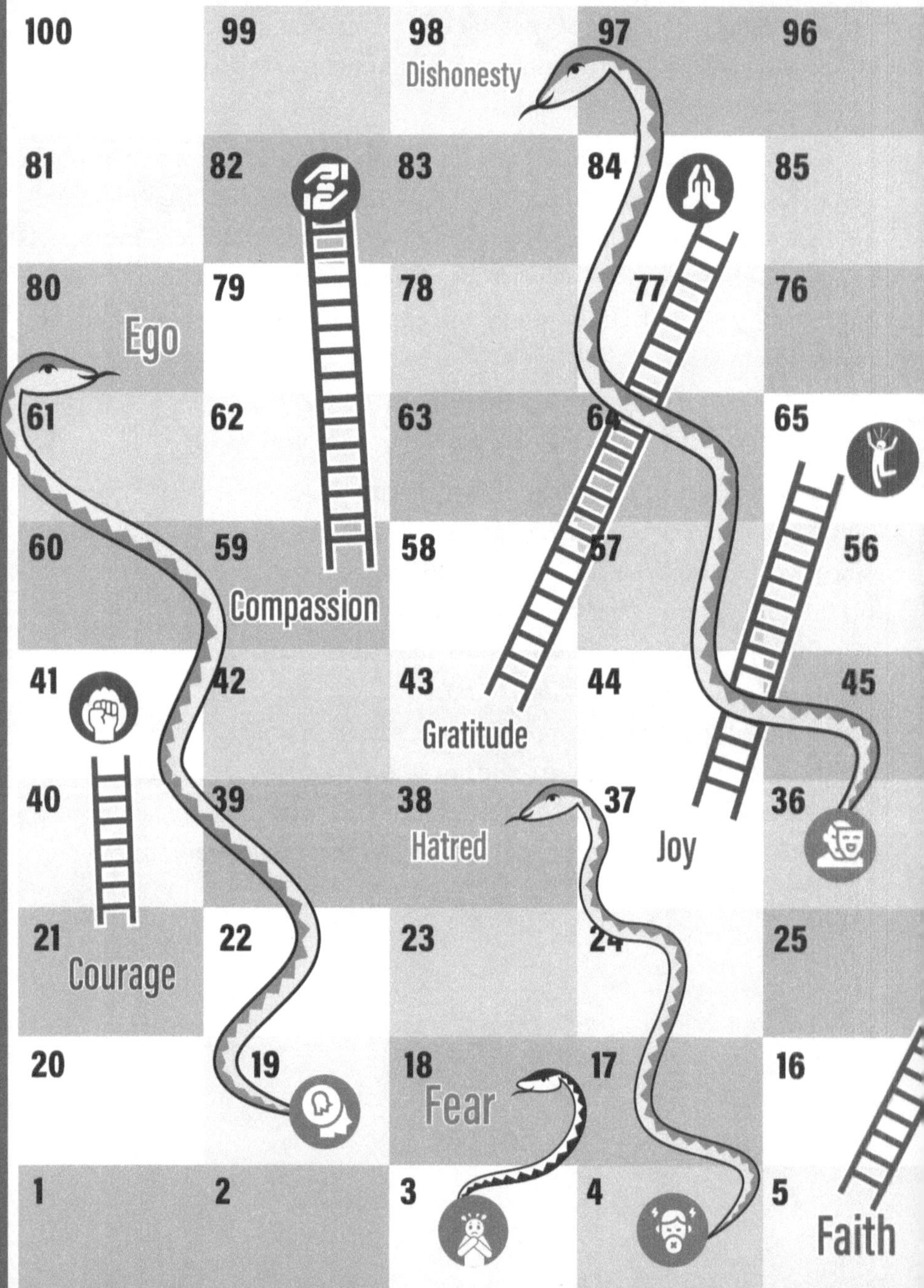

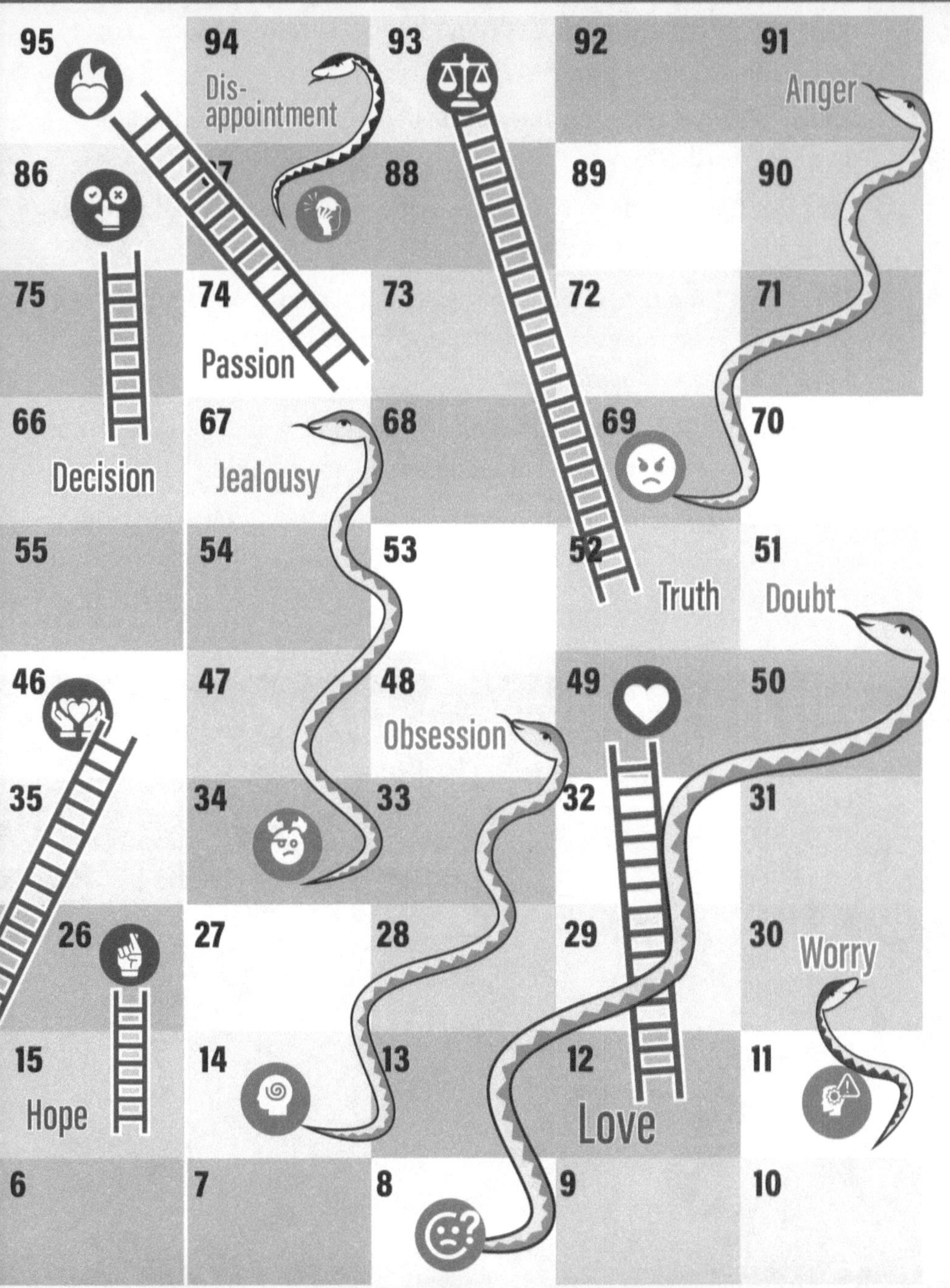
95
94 Dis-appointment
93
92
91 Anger
86
88
89
90
75
74 Passion
73
72
71
66 Decision
67 Jealousy
68
69
70
55
54
53
52 Truth
51 Doubt
46
47
48 Obsession
49
50
35
34
33
32
31
26
27
28
29
30 Worry
15 Hope
14
13
12 Love
11
6
7
8
9
10

Cultivating Positive Energy for Growth

Achieving excellence is not just about outward accomplishments. It's about nurturing the right energy within yourself. The thoughts, words, and actions you project affect both your personal growth and the people around you.

Think of this process like the interaction between the **Sun (Soul)**, **Moon (Mind)**, and **Earth (Body)**:

The Sun (Soul) radiates constant energy, much like our soul provides inner strength and guidance.

The Moon (Mind) reflects the Sun's light, just as our mind reflects our soul's energy. When aligned, the mind experiences clarity and peace. When disconnected, it becomes restless.

The Earth (Body) grounds us in the physical world, providing the stability we need to bring our thoughts and actions to life.

Just as these celestial bodies work together, balancing our soul, mind, and body helps us cultivate positive energy, leading to personal and social growth.

Practical Tips for Managing Positive and Negative Energy

In today's fast-paced world, staying connected to positive energy can be a challenge. We face distractions, stress, and negativity that can drain our emotional and mental energy. However, we can take conscious steps to manage this.

Here are a few tips to help you stay aligned with positive energy:

Mindfulness Practices: Regular meditation or mindfulness exercises help you stay centered and aware of your inner energy.

Gratitude Journaling: Writing down what you're grateful for every day shifts your focus from what's lacking to what's abundant, fostering positive energy.

Empathy Exercises: Practice empathy by actively putting yourself in others' shoes. This helps reduce negativity and promotes understanding and kindness.

By managing your energy proactively, you not only enhance your personal well-being but also influence the environment and people around you for the better.

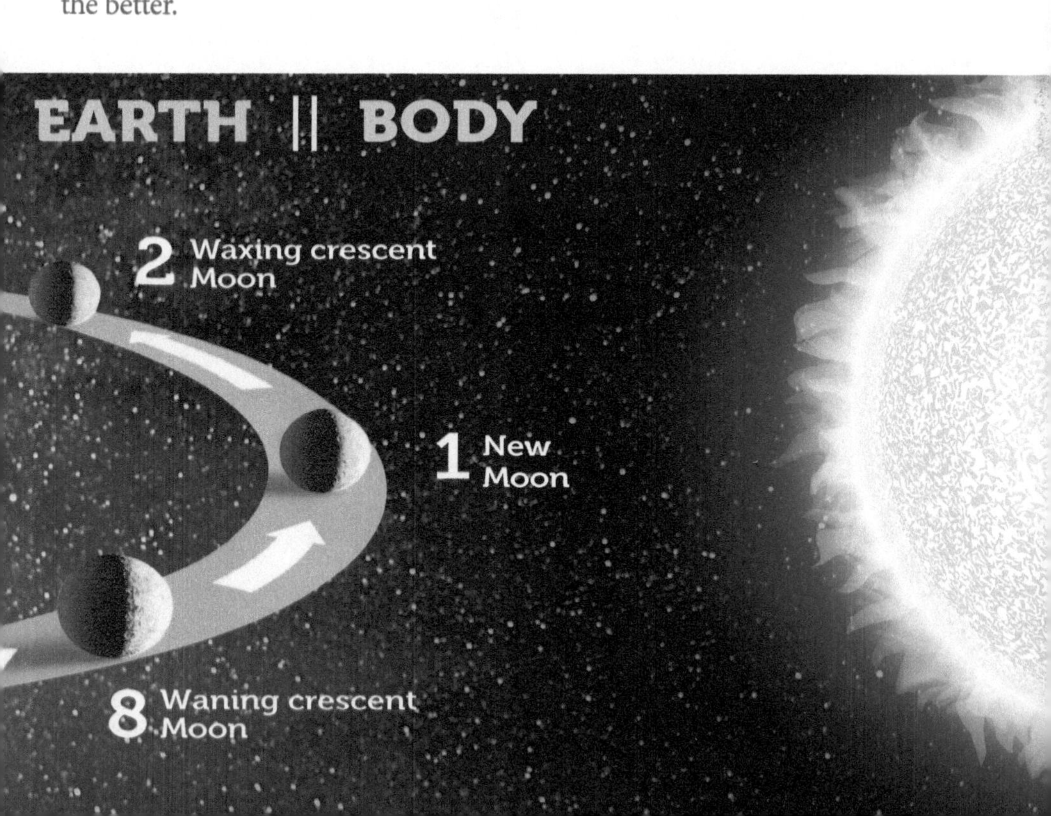

> 66
>
> *Magic happens when you focus your inner power on the change you want to see.*
>
> 99

– Bangambiki Habyarimana

Lunar Wisdom

> 66
>
> *The moon glows in the light of the Sun but fades in the darkness when it turns away. Just like the mind shines with joy when in harmony with the soul, and sinks into sorrow when it loses their connection.*
>
> 99

-Rajeev Kharyal

Section-B
Summary
(Chapters 11-15)

1. Social Quotient and Its Role:

This section explains the importance of social intelligence, called Social Quotient (SQ), along with IQ (Intelligence Quotient) and EQ (Emotional Quotient). True success is shown as the combination of emotional intelligence and a sense of responsibility toward society, not just personal achievements.

2. Evolution of Social Intelligence:

The section traces the history of social intelligence from early ideas to modern interpretations. It highlights empathy and action as key parts of high SQ, showing how socially intelligent people can handle complex situations and inspire positive change.

3. Contrasting Mindsets:

A comparison is made between two approaches to life: segment 13, which focuses on self-interest, and segment 3, which is centered on compassion. This shows the difference between selfish ambition and caring for others in achieving success.

4. Impact of High SQ Individuals:

People with high SQ, who prioritize improving society, are discussed with examples. The text emphasizes how personal growth and social improvement are connected, and how these individuals drive collective progress.

5. Altruism and Social Change:

The importance of altruism, honesty, and social intelligence in creating positive change is emphasized. These are presented as practical tools that can transform both individuals and communities.

6. The Triad of Excellence:

The section introduces the idea of excellence through IQ, EQ, and SQ. It explains that progress is possible, but there is also the risk of setbacks, like in the game of snakes and ladders.

7. Key Takeaway:

The main message is the importance of developing social intelligence, practicing kindness, and embracing a sense of responsibility for the greater good. Readers are encouraged to aim for making a positive impact on the world, as true fulfillment comes from helping others, not just personal success.

The Struggles of a Distracted Mind

Despite the wealth of information available to us, many people struggle to make meaningful changes in their lives. Why do we find it so hard to focus on what truly matters? The answer is simple: we are overwhelmed by the constant flood of thoughts.

Understanding Our Inner Self

To delve deeper into the workings of the mind, it is helpful to explore the concept of the subtle body, which consists of 19 key components that govern our inner experiences and energy flow.

5 Organs of knowledge
Eyes, Ears, Nose, Tongue, Skin

5 Organs of action
Speech, Hands, Legs, Genitals, Anus

4 Internal Organs
Mind, Intellect, Memory, Ego

5 Pranas
Prana, Apana, Vyana, Udana, Samana

The Five Organs of Knowledge:

These are the sensory faculties—sight, hearing, touch, taste, and smell—that allow us to perceive and understand the world.

The Five Organs of Action:

These faculties enable interaction with our environment, such as speaking, moving, grasping, and expressing ourselves through physical actions.

The Five Pranas:

These are life-sustaining energies that regulate vital functions like breathing, digestion, circulation, and overall vitality.

The Four Aspects of the Mind:

Mind: Facilitates thinking, perception, and processing of information.

Intellect: Responsible for reasoning, analyzing, and decision-making.

Memory: Stores past experiences and accumulated knowledge.

Ego: Creates a sense of individuality and self-identity.

Together, these components shape our inner and outer experiences, influencing our thoughts, emotions, actions, and ultimately, how we perceive and engage with life.

Understanding the Structure of the Mind:

A Path to Grasping Its Nuances

To truly understand the mind's complexities, it is essential to first grasp its basic structure. The mind operates as a dual control system, comprising the conscious mind and the subconscious mind, each playing distinct yet interconnected roles in shaping our lives.

The Conscious and Subconscious Mind: A Dual Control System

The mind functions in two main parts: The Conscious Mind and The Subconscious Mind.

in book **"The Power of Your Subconscious Mind"**, Joseph Murphy beautifully shared the below explaination of garden analogy to describe the dual role of Mind in form of conscious mind and sub-conscious mind.

The Garden Analogy:

Conscious Mind (The Gardener):

The conscious mind is like a gardener. It decides which seeds to plant in the soil. These seeds are your thoughts, beliefs, and ideas. Every thought you focus on, every belief you hold, and every mental image you cultivate acts like a seed being planted in the garden of your mind.

Subconscious Mind (The Fertile Soil):

The subconscious mind is like the fertile soil of the garden. It doesn't question or discriminate the seeds it receives. Whether the seeds are of positive thoughts (like success, happiness, health) or negative ones (like fear, doubt, failure), the soil will nurture and grow them. It simply follows the gardener's instructions and brings those seeds to fruition.

Key Lesson from the Analogy:

- If the gardener plants weeds (negative, self-defeating thoughts), the soil will grow them as vigorously as it would grow flowers.

- If the gardener plants flowers (positive, constructive thoughts), the soil will help them thrive.

The conscious mind must be careful about what thoughts it allows into the subconscious mind. The subconscious mind cannot distinguish between good and bad thoughts—it simply acts on the instructions it's given.

This analogy emphasizes the importance of mindfulness, as the quality of your "garden" (your life) depends on the seeds (thoughts and beliefs) you choose to plant

These two parts create a feedback loop:

Thoughts -> Feelings -> Actions -> Results

To bring about meaningful change in life, one must start by transforming their thoughts. Positive and empowering thoughts create a ripple effect, leading to positive emotions, constructive actions, and improved results

The Monkey Mind: A Restless Mental State

A common mental state that disrupts focus is known as the "monkey mind," where thoughts jump from one to the next without ever settling.

It is my understanding that "The modern world focuses on process excellence, but we should also focus on human excellence, which helps us to move from a monkey mind to a balanced mind."

The restless mind leads to disorganization, stress, and a constant sense of distraction.

Calming the Monkey Mind: Simple Techniques for Mental Clarity

Thankfully, the monkey mind can be tamed through mindfulness and simple practices:

Mindful Breathing: Focus on your breath for 5–10 minutes daily to bring your mind into the present moment.

Thought Journaling: Writing down distracting thoughts helps release their hold on your mind.

Gratitude Practice: Reflecting on three things you're grateful for each day shifts your focus toward positivity and peace.

These small but consistent actions bring a sense of calm and focus to a scattered mind.

In today's time , there are also other discreet practices to improve from a scattered mind situation as per the specific need of individuals.

The Theta State: A Gateway to Manifestation

The theta state (4-8 Hz) occurs before sleep and after waking, making it ideal for manifestation and setting intentions.

By tapping into the theta state, you can:

- **Amplify intentions:** Increase the power of your desires.

- **Access the subconscious mind:** Unlock its secrets.

- **Boost creativity:** Enhance imagination and inspiration.

A Step-by-Step Guide to Manifestation

1. Set intentions: Reflect on desires before sleep or after waking.

2. Visualize: Imagine achieving goals.

3. Repeat affirmations: Reinforce intentions with positive affirmations.

4. Let go: Release attachment to specific outcomes.

The Placebo Effect

One of the most compelling demonstrations of the mind's influence is the placebo effect. People often experience genuine improvements in health or well-being from treatments that lack medical efficacy, solely because they believe in their effectiveness.

This phenomenon highlights the deep connection between mind and body. Positive thoughts and beliefs can trigger tangible, beneficial changes, underscoring the transformative power of the mind.

Few examples of undesirable reasons of Distracted Mind

Example 1 :

A "13 mindset" tends to let problems linger within the system until they are noticed by senior management. When eventually prompted to address the issue, individuals with a "13 mindset" quickly adopt solutions but keep them to themselves, presenting these as unique skills or insights to showcase their superiority.

This approach prioritizes self-promotion and recognition over genuine problem-solving—a stark difference from the collaborative and straightforward approach of a "3 mindset," which values shared growth and transparency.

Example 2 :

Sometimes, problems are self-created, particularly due to prevalent bad habits in the corporate and professional world. One such habit is the "Mindset 13" phenomenon, where individuals, upon realizing they cannot outperform their "Mindset 3" competitors, resort to destructive tactics. Instead of enhancing their own skills and capabilities—a hallmark of Mindset 3 individuals—they fall into a jealousy-driven loop. They attempt to hinder their competitors' progress through false allegations and other damaging strategies.

This behavior eventually traps Mindset 13 individuals in a vicious cycle of stress and negativity, which is entirely self-inflicted. The way out of such problems lies in surrounding oneself with people of higher qualities and values. These individuals can sense subtle changes in attitude and provide timely guidance for course correction before it's too late.

True self-introspection is also essential. It often reveals that the root causes of depression are envy, over-ambition, unrealistic goals beyond one's capabilities, and similar tendencies. Recognizing and addressing these issues can pave the way for personal growth and a more fulfilling professional journey.

Other Scenerios :

Chapter 25 is section of Self assessments which greatly help to identify the various ways which result into a Distracted Mind.

Later 3A framework is also disucssed where through Aware, Acceptance & Action , it can bring back to Balance mind with consistent efforts through SMART Actions.

Managing the Mind:

The "3 Segment" Concept They've learned to filter out distractions and focus on what truly matters. This allows them to remain calm and effective even in stressful situations.

Simplicity in Thought Management: The Empty Soap Packet Problem

A renowned soap company in a developed country faced a multimilliondollar lawsuit when a customer found an empty soap packet. Determined to prevent further losses, the management hired top-rated consultants to investigate and find a permanent solution at the manufacturing plant.

The consultants spent days exploring high-tech solutions, including laser beams, but couldn't conclude a foolproof method. Meanwhile, the plant foreman asked his manager about the consultants' visit. After understanding the problem, the foreman suggested a simple solution: installing a high-velocity exhaust fan above the packed soap assembly line. This would blow away any empty packets, eliminating the issue.

When the manager shared the foreman's solution with the management, they felt embarrassed and realized that not every problem requires a complex solution. Sometimes, the answer lies in simple, practical thinking. The company implemented the foreman's solution, and the problem vanished.

Just as the soap company's issue was solved by a simple, practical solution, calming the monkey mind and finding clarity often involves addressing the root cause with balanced thinking. The key is to avoid overcomplicating problems with unnecessary mental clutter and instead focus on practical, grounded solutions.

Solutions are often close to the problem itself, and a balanced mind can uncover them with simplicity and clarity.

Those with a "3 mindset" approach problems calmly and effectively, finding solutions without unnecessary stress, restlessness by filtering out the distractions and related thoughts through FOCUS mind.

This is one key difference between "3 mindset " and "13 mindset" which makes 1st as Gold and 2nd as Silver category on analogy understanding on Human excellence.

Conclusion: Finding Clarity Through Simplicity

The path to a clear, focused mind doesn't require eliminating thoughts or chasing complex solutions. Instead, it's about embracing simple, mindful practices that help us focus on what matters. By guiding our thoughts intentionally and avoiding unnecessary distractions, we can cultivate mental clarity and live a life driven by peace and purpose.

Chapter 17

The Inner Focus

India has long been a cradle of wisdom, home to sages whose insights have left a lasting legacy of inner peace and understanding. These enlightened individuals lived in harmony with nature, long before modern cities rose across the land. They recognized a fundamental truth: everything in the natural world is interconnected. This realization shaped their pursuit of personal awakening.

To these sages, true happiness was not found in material wealth but in embracing the balance of life. Their observations of nature's harmony taught them that respecting the connections between all living things was key to lasting joy. In contrast to modern society, where we often chase external pleasures, they found fulfillment in understanding the deeper, spiritual ties that bind us all.

Over centuries, many of these sages traveled beyond India, spreading the wisdom of inner focus and spiritual growth to the Western world. Their teachings resonated deeply, attracting millions of followers who sought guidance in transforming their lives.

Following are two among those numerous Sages Who Inspired the millions worldwide with their teachings:

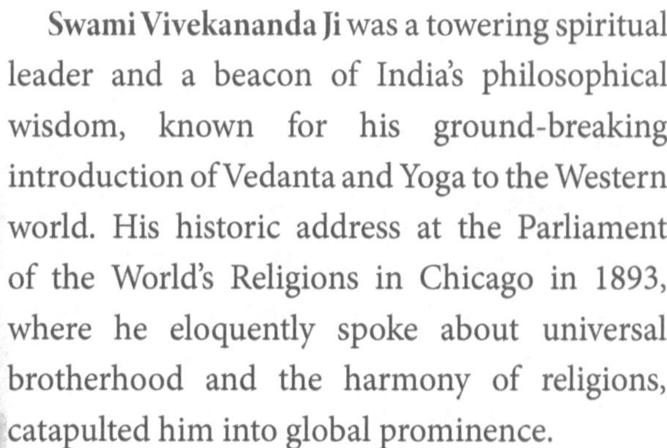

Swami Vivekananda Ji was a towering spiritual leader and a beacon of India's philosophical wisdom, known for his ground-breaking introduction of Vedanta and Yoga to the Western world. His historic address at the Parliament of the World's Religions in Chicago in 1893, where he eloquently spoke about universal brotherhood and the harmony of religions, catapulted him into global prominence.

A disciple of Sri Ramakrishna Paramahamsa, Swami Vivekananda's vision was deeply rooted in the idea that spirituality and action go hand in hand. He founded the Ramakrishna Mission, which continues to serve humanity through education, healthcare, and humanitarian work. His philosophy of self-empowerment, spiritual growth, and the interconnectedness of life has left an indelible mark on the world, encouraging millions to rise above limitations and realize their divine potential.

Swami Satyanand Ji Maharaj: A Visionary Spiritual Luminary

Swami Satyanand Ji Maharaj is celebrated as a profound spiritual teacher whose contributions to Hindu philosophy continue to illuminate the path to liberation (moksha) for countless seekers. He authored 11 seminal Hindu scriptures, including Ramayana, Gita, Upanishad, Bhakti Prakash, and Amrit Vani. These works offer timeless wisdom, addressing the complexities of human life with clarity and guidance rooted in spiritual principles. His writings bridge the ancient teachings of Hinduism with the challenges of contemporary life, making spirituality accessible to individuals from all backgrounds.

Swami Satyanand Ji's approach to spiritual growth is distinctive for its simplicity and practicality. Rejecting overly complex rituals or ascetic practices, he emphasized methods that are easy to adopt for modern professionals and people engaged in worldly responsibilities. His teachings help seekers transcend the "law of gravity"—a metaphor for the illusions and attachments that keep us bound to material existence. By advocating a balanced approach to life, he showed how one can integrate spiritual awakening with everyday duties, enabling harmony between worldly obligations and inner progress.

Timeless Relevance of His Teachings

What distinguishes Swami Satyanand Ji is his profound understanding of human nature and his exceptional ability to present spirituality in a manner that is both relatable and accessible to people from all walks of life. He recognized the struggles of modern life and offered solutions that blend ancient wisdom with practical application. His teachings empower individuals to cultivate self-awareness, inner peace, and a higher purpose while remaining engaged in their personal and professional lives.

The universal appeal of his works lies in their ability to inspire people to seek a deeper connection with their true selves while honoring their responsibilities. Swami Satyanand Ji's philosophy highlights that liberation is not limited to renunciates but is achievable for anyone willing to introspect, adopt discipline, and pursue a path of righteousness. His contributions stand as a beacon of hope and guidance for those striving to balance the demands of the material world with the pursuit of spiritual fulfilment. Their teachings remind us of the enduring value of connecting with our inner selves, living in harmony with the world, and embracing the interconnectedness of all existence

Arjuna's questions in the Gita reflect timeless human doubts and challenges that resonate with people of all eras. Lord Krishna's responses were designed to clear Arjuna's confusion, helping him see the right path and take decisive action. These teachings, interpreted by Swami Satyanand Ji Maharaj, offer valuable guidance for modern seekers from any walk of life. The insights below explore key principles for developing Intellectual (IQ), Emotional (EQ), and Spiritual (SQ) Quotients:

IQ (Intellectual Quotient)

Wrong thinking is the only problem in life:

How we think shapes how we experience life. Fear, negativity, or wrong assumptions make small problems feel overwhelming. Clear, positive thinking helps us see challenges as they are and solve them wisely—like cleaning a dirty lens to see clearly.

Right knowledge is the ultimate solution to all our problems:

True knowledge is more than facts—it's the wisdom to understand what matters most. Whether at work or in life, solving problems becomes easier when we have the right perspective. Think of knowledge as the instruction manual for navigating life.

Choosing the right over the pleasant is a sign of power:

The easy way often feels good in the moment but rarely lasts. Choosing what is right, even when it's hard, leads to long-term growth. For example, acting with honesty and integrity may take effort now but earns trust and respect that endure.

Never give up on yourself:

Life's challenges are not failures but lessons that make you stronger. Like a tree weathering storms to grow taller, persistence helps us turn setbacks into success. Trust your potential—it's your greatest strength.

EQ (Emotional Quotient)

Live what you learn:

Knowledge is only useful when applied. For instance, learning about kindness means nothing if you don't show patience and empathy in daily life. Practice what you know to inspire others and grow as a person.

Being good is a reward in itself:

Acts of goodness, like helping someone or being honest, bring inner peace. You don't need applause; the joy of doing the right thing is enough. Goodness, like planting flowers, adds beauty to life without asking for anything in return.

Live a lifestyle that matches your vision:

Your daily habits shape your future. If your dream is to be successful, adopt routines that support it—like learning new skills, staying disciplined, or taking care of your health. Small steps every day lead to big achievements.

Absorb your mind in the higher:

Focus on goals that uplift you—whether it's improving yourself, helping others, or finding peace. A higher purpose gives life meaning and helps you stay above petty worries, like a kite that rises higher with the wind.

SQ (Spiritual Quotient)

Value your blessings:

Gratitude shifts your focus from what you lack to what you already have. Take time to appreciate your health, relationships, and small joys. Gratitude turns ordinary moments into a source of happiness.

Selflessness is the only way to progress and prosperity:

True growth happens when you help others. For example, when leaders support their teams, everyone—including the leader—succeeds. Like a river nourishing everything in its path, selflessness creates lasting abundance.

Renounce the ego of individuality and rejoice in the bliss of infinity:

Clinging to the ego isolates us and creates conflict. Letting go of selfishness helps you feel part of something bigger—a team, a family, or the universe. Like a stream merging with the ocean, you lose nothing but gain boundless peace.

Every act can be an act of prayer:

Any task, done with focus and care, becomes meaningful. Whether you're working, helping someone, or spending time with family, doing it with mindfulness turns ordinary actions into something sacred.

Mastering the Senses for Inner Awareness

Humans experience life through the five senses: sight, hearing, touch, smell, and taste. These senses are our primary tools for perceiving the world, but they are also the gateways to deeper awareness. The ancient sages understood this and believed that by mastering their senses, they could attain greater clarity, peace, and understanding of life.

They teach us that by tuning in to our senses and the world around us, we can sharpen our focus and cultivate a deeper connection with ourselves and our surroundings. This heightened awareness is the foundation of true inner focus.

The Voltage of Awareness

> *Just as power transmission is stepped down from higher to lower voltage for efficiency and safety, our body's functions work in a similar hierarchy. Our senses operate at the highest level of awareness, showing us the way.*

— *Rajeev Kharyal*

Focus as the Key to Mastery:
Lessons from Sachin Tendulkar and Arjuna

Every child in India knows the name Sachin Tendulkar, a cricket legend who mastered his craft through not just endless practice, but smart, focused practice. Even he, with all his talent, experienced nervousness before matches. What set him apart was his ability to maintain laser-like focus during each game. Rather than practicing aimlessly, Tendulkar focused on refining specific skills, always aligning his practice with a clear goal.

During matches, his focus was evident in every ball bowled. Like Arjuna in the Mahabharata, whose sole focus was the eye of the fish during an archery challenge, Tendulkar blocked out distractions, honing in only on what mattered in that moment. Both Tendulkar and Arjuna exemplify the power of unwavering focus in achieving excellence.

Holistic Learning: The Guru-Shishya Tradition

The power of focus is not a new discovery. For centuries, Indian sages and teachers (gurus) have been practicing and teaching mindfulness and focused learning. In ancient India, the guru-shishya (teacher-student) system was the foundation of education. Gurus imparted not only academic knowledge but also life skills, all while fostering a deep, respectful bond with their students.

These gurukuls (traditional schools) emphasized holistic education, with gurus focusing deeply on their own thoughts before passing their wisdom to their students. This approach didn't involve a strict curriculum but instead concentrated on teaching through immersion, using all five senses. Students learned self-defense, medicine, language, and how to live harmoniously with nature, engaging both the mind and the senses in a complete learning experience.

The secret behind the effectiveness of the guru-shishya system was focus. The gurus themselves had mastered the art of mental clarity and taught their students to do the same. By encouraging deep concentration, they helped their students cultivate inner awareness, discipline, and harmony with their surroundings.

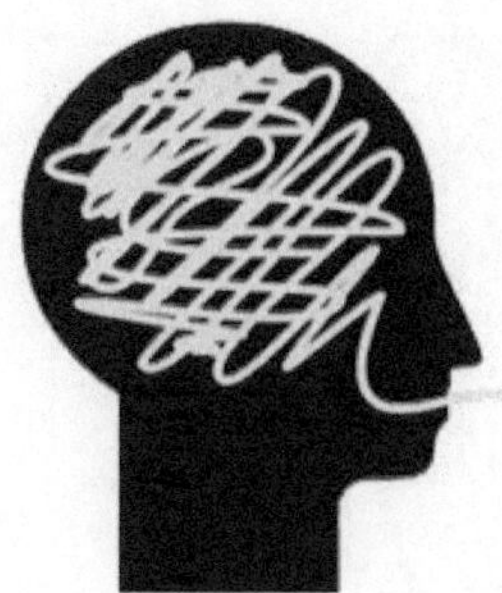

The Hidden Power of Focus: Unlocking Success

In today's world, focus is often an overlooked skill. In his book Focus: The Hidden Driver of Excellence, Daniel Goleman emphasizes that focus is not an inherent trait but a skill that can be cultivated and strengthened over time. Just like a muscle, focus grows with practice.

Focus Formula

Electrical Energy = Current × Voltage.
Human Energy = Thought × Focus.

Just like electrical energy works best with lower current and higher voltage, human energy is most effective when we keep our thoughts clear and simple while focusing on what truly matters. By reducing distractions and concentrating on important goals, we can achieve more and discover a deeper sense of purpose in life. A focused mind turns potential into progress.

The Energy of Emotions

Unlock the Power Within

Electrical Energy Loss = (Current)^2 × Conductor Resistance
Human Energy Loss = (Thoughts)^2 × Negative Emotions

Just as conductor resistance hinders electrical flow, negative emotions like jealousy, fear, and anxiety block your focus, causing human energy loss.

Transform your emotions, unlock your power.

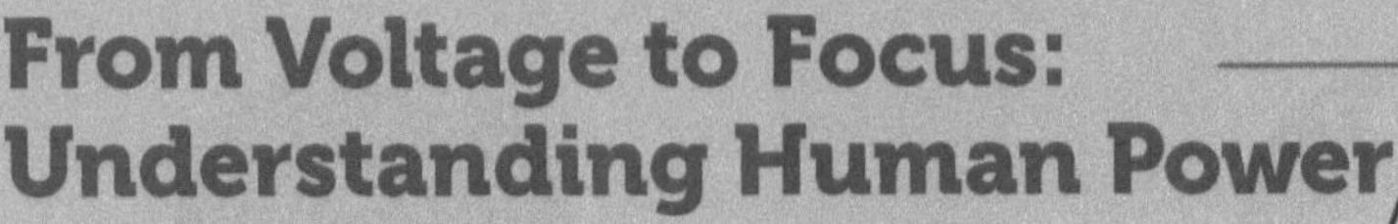

From Voltage to Focus: Understanding Human Power

The Focus Scale serves as a powerful metaphorical tool, much like the visual acuity test, in understanding the clarity and focus of our thoughts.

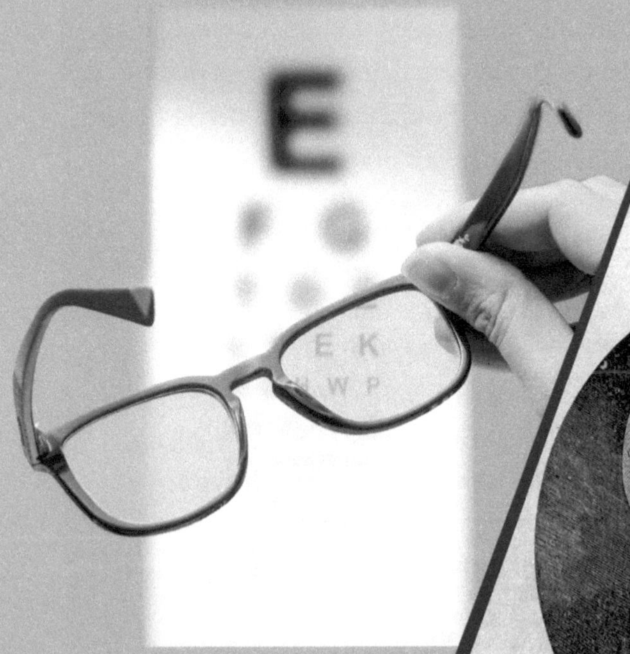

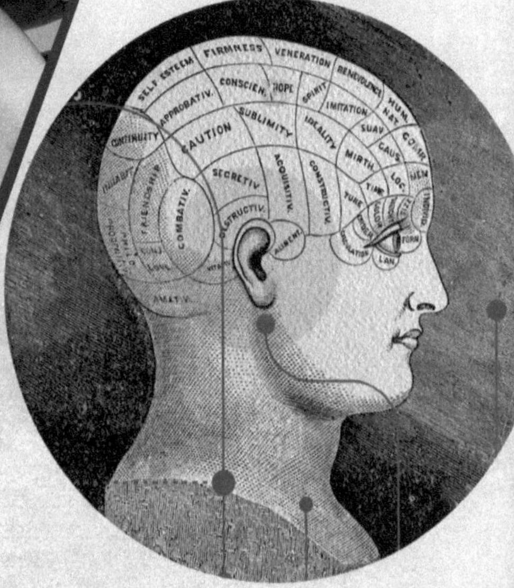

Just as corrective lenses help improve vision, individuals in 84% /13% band require strategies and practices to enhance their mental clarity and focus, such as mindfulness techniques, prioritization skills, and decluttering methods.

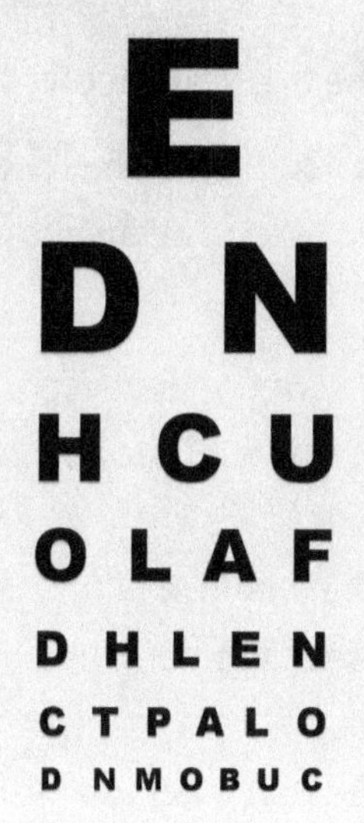

Type of Insights ▼	Pathways to Insights ▼	Eye Focus Level	Mind Per Day Thoughts
		6/6	6,000
SQ Gratitude Truth Faith	• Every act can be an act of prayer • Renounce the ego of individuality & rejoice in the bliss of infinity • Selflessness is the only way to progress & prosperity • Value your blessings	6/9 6/12	9,000 12,000
EQ Passion Compassion Love Joy	• Absorb your mind in the higher. • Live a lifestyle that matches your vision. • Being good is a reward in itself. • Live what you learn	6/18 6/24	18,000 24,000
IQ Hope Courage Decision	• Never give up on yourself. • Choosing the right over the pleasant is a sign of power. • Right knowledge is the ultimate solution to all our problems. • Wrong thinking is the only problem in life.	6/36 6/60	36,000 60,000

Here's a detailed explanation of the 6/6 scale acuity test:

The 6/6 scale is a measure of visual acuity, which is the sharpness and clarity of vision. The scale is used to assess the smallest letters that a person can read at a distance of 6 meters.

The numbers on the 6/6 scale represent the distance (in meters) at which a person with normal vision can read the corresponding line. For example:

- **6/6:** Normal vision, can read the smallest letters at 6 meters.
- **6/9:** Can read letters at 6 meters that a person with normal vision can read at 9 meters.
- **6/12:** Can read letters at 6 meters that a person with normal vision can read at 12 meters.

Just as the eye chart progressively challenges our vision, the Focus Thoughts Scale challenges our ability to concentrate and maintain clarity amidst the noise of our thoughts. At the beginning of the test, where smaller letters require normal vision, only individuals in the 3% band can read with ease, navigating through 6/6, 6/9, and 6/12 levels with clarity.

While those in the 13% band can read through 6/18 and 6/24 levels and not below these bands.

However, individuals in the 84% band read through 6/36 and 6/60 levels, but unable to read below these levels even where letters are yet large, signifying a critical loss of focus and clarity, similar to the overwhelming clutter of thoughts they experience.

Conclusion: Focus as the Path to Inner Peace and Success

In summary, the power of inner focus is central to achieving both personal mastery and peace of mind. Whether we look to ancient Indian sages, modern athletes like Sachin Tendulkar, or the wisdom passed down through the guru-shishya tradition, the message is clear: focus is the key to success, growth, and happiness.

Chapter 18

From Chaos to Clarity

Have you ever felt overwhelmed by a cluttered mind? Personal issues, work, and constant distractions from social media can scatter your thoughts and make it hard to focus. In today's fast-paced world, mental clutter is common. It's easy to get lost in a sea of thoughts, making it difficult to prioritize and stay calm.

But **here's the good news**: you can clear away the mental chaos. By learning to manage your thoughts, you can sharpen your focus, bring clarity to your life, and live with a greater sense of purpose.

The Link Between Focus and Clarity

One key lesson is that the more thoughts we juggle, the less focus we can give to each one. Imagine trying to read a blurred eye chart—when the letters are unclear, it's hard to read anything properly. The same thing happens in your mind. When too many thoughts compete for attention, nothing gets the focus it needs, and you end up feeling scattered.

But when you narrow your focus, you give more energy to each thought, allowing you to make real progress. Often, we waste mental energy by overthinking—rehashing past mistakes or worrying about future problems. This overthinking distracts us from the present moment, the only time we can take action.

By letting go of unnecessary thoughts and focusing on what truly matters, you can regain clarity and achieve more with less effort.

The Power of Now: From Chaos to Clarity

Life can be broken down into three parts: the past, the present, and the future. But the present is where everything happens. The past has already unfolded, and while it holds lessons, it can't be changed. The future holds possibilities, but it's still uncertain. The present is the only place where you can take action and create change.

So how do we balance these three parts of life to reduce mental clutter and increase clarity?

The book titled "The Power of Now" by Eckhart Tolle beautifully explains it

The Past: Learn Without Dwelling

The past is valuable for the lessons it teaches, but dwelling on it too much can hold you back.

Learn from experience: Use the past to inform your present decisions, but don't let it consume you. Take the lessons, leave the regrets. Let go of guilt: Worrying about past mistakes adds to mental clutter. Forgive yourself, learn from missteps, and move forward. Avoid nostalgia traps: It's comforting to think about the good times, but living in the past stops you from fully engaging with the present.

Tip: Think of the past like a rearview mirror—glance at it for guidance, but don't stare at it, or you'll miss the road ahead.

The Future: Plan Without Stress

The future holds endless possibilities, but excessive focus on what might happen creates anxiety. Rhonda Byrne's book "The Secret" beautifully conveys that "Think what you want, don't think what you don't want." A crucial understanding of the Law of Attraction is that thinking "I shouldn't fail in exams" actually means you want to fail in exams. So, avoid thinking about what you don't want.

Set goals, but act today: Having goals is important, but remember that progress happens in the present. Every step you take today moves you closer to your future aspirations.

Avoid over-planning: While preparing for the future is wise, stressing about what's beyond your control adds unnecessary mental noise. Focus on the actions you can take today.

Don't wait for "perfect timing": Waiting for the ideal moment often leads to procrastination. Start now and adjust as you go.

Tip: Think of the future like a GPS—it gives direction, but don't fixate on the destination and forget to enjoy the journey.

The Present: Your Moment of Power

The present is where life truly happens. When we focus on the present, we free ourselves from the weight of past regrets and future anxieties. Clarity thrives in the now.

Mindful action: Being fully present in what you're doing helps you make better decisions and enjoy life more deeply. Engage with the moment: Whether it's enjoying a conversation or appreciating a sunset, being present lets you experience life's meaningful moments. Reduce stress: Focusing on the present helps lower stress by shifting attention away from the past and future.

Tip: The present is your most powerful tool. By focusing on today, you shape tomorrow and find peace with yesterday.

Finding Balance Between Past, Present, and Future

A balanced life means learning from the past, planning for the future, but living fully in the present. Here's how to keep perspective:

The past is a rearview mirror: Glance at it for guidance, but don't get stuck looking back. The future is a GPS: It gives direction, but don't let the destination overshadow your current journey. The present is the road beneath you: This is where life happens, where decisions are made, and where clarity is found.

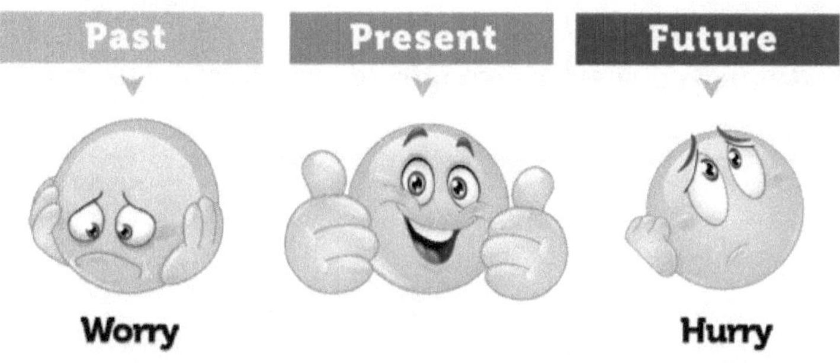

Conclusion: Focus on Now for a Clearer Future

While the past and future are important, your true power lies in the present. By managing your thoughts and focusing on the now, you bring clarity to your life. The past offers lessons, the future holds potential, but the present is where you take action to shape your destiny.

Clarity comes when you let go of mental clutter, narrow your focus, and fully engage with the present. Let the past guide you, the future inspire you, and the present be your stage for transformation.

The Gift of Now

> **The past holds lessons, yet clinging brings worry; the future offers hope, but chasing creates hurry. The present is a gift, unfolding moment by moment, inviting us to experience life in its fullest bloom.**

— Rajeev Kharyal

The Power of Now

> **The past is gone, having moved through the present, and the future will also arrive in the now. It's in this present moment that real actions and karmas come to life. Let's be fully present to make the most of every moment.**

— Rajeev Kharyal

The Digest of Wisdom

> **"Information is food for the mind, and understanding is digestion. Feed wisely; digest deeply to fuel your success".**

— Rajeev Kharyal

Chapter 19

The Darwinian Selection

Charles Darwin's idea of "survival of the fittest" isn't just about nature—it also applies to some of the toughest exams in India, like the Indian Administrative Service (IAS) and MBA programs. If you've ever seen interviews with top candidates, you'll notice that passing the written exams is just the start of their journey.

As Darwin said

> *It is not the strongest or the most intelligent who survive, but those who can adapt to change.*

Success in these exams isn't just about being smart. The final stages, such as interviews, test how well candidates can handle change. These evaluations focus on personality, leadership, problem-solving, and emotional intelligence.

Just like in nature, success here isn't about being the smartest person in the room. It's about being adaptable, resilient, and emotionally strong. The best candidates are those who can face challenges, not just those with high test scores.

Parental Expectations and Adaptability

In today's fast-paced world, parents should expand their focus beyond academic success. High grades, though valuable, are no longer the sole indicators of future success. As educator Ken Robinson famously noted, "Creativity is as important in education as literacy, and we should treat it with the same importance." Instead of emphasizing only high marks, parents should foster a range of skills in their children, including creativity, problem-solving, and emotional intelligence.

One way parents can nurture adaptability in children is by drawing on teachings from classic Indian texts like the Ramayana, Mahabharata, and Bhagavad Gita. These texts offer timeless stories and lessons on balancing intellect, emotions, and social skills, instilling values like empathy, resilience, and ethical decision-making.

A Holistic Approach in Education

Educational institutions, especially top colleges, should prioritize the comprehensive development of students. While these institutions often excel at preparing students for prestigious roles, they must also address students' mental and emotional well-being. A tool like a "Virtues Wellness Scale" could help monitor students' emotional health, alleviating issues like stress and low self-esteem that arise from academic pressure.

Parents invest significantly in their children's education, aiming for well-rounded growth. Schools can support this by offering more than academic training. Implementing a comprehensive report card that evaluates personal growth, emotional health, and overall development—not just grades—would be a meaningful step.

Adaptability: The Key to Success

Albert Einstein once said,

> **66**
> *The measure of intelligence is the ability to change.*
> **99**

True success stems from flexibility and openness to new challenges, requiring a blend of intellectual, emotional, and practical skills. Parents play a crucial role by encouraging their children to develop diverse abilities to navigate an ever-changing world.

Holistic Excellence in All Areas of Life

Achieving balanced excellence extends beyond academics, influencing all areas of life—from sports to relationships, work, and the arts:

Sports: Top athletes possess both physical and mental strength. A marathon runner, for instance, needs physical endurance and the mental grit to push through challenges.

Arts: Creativity requires emotional connection and persistence. Great artists, musicians, and writers resonate with audiences and demonstrate dedication to their craft.

Relationships: Success in relationships depends on empathy, communication, and adaptability. Strong relationships flourish when people work through challenges together.

Workplace: Employers value creative problem-solvers who can collaborate effectively, adapt to change, and manage stress.

In every domain, a balanced approach that integrates multiple skills leads to lasting success, illustrating that excellence requires more than single-minded focus on any one area

> *The pursuit of Human Excellence is a journey: from being 'Right,' guided by IQ (Intelligent Quotient), to becoming 'More Right' by integrating EQ (Emotional Quotient), and ultimately striving for the 'Absolute Right' through SQ (Social Quotient) — with righteous choices lighting the way at every step.*
>
> *— Rajeev Kharyal*

Fostering Holistic Development

Success in life is a combination of intelligence, emotional strength, and practical abilities. Schools, families, and workplaces should promote this balance and help people develop all these areas.

"Survival of the fittest" doesn't mean being the strongest or smartest. It means creating an environment where everyone can grow and develop their unique talents. By focusing on holistic development, we prepare individuals to face challenges with confidence and resilience.

Story of Resilience: Bhagat Singh 

A great example of holistic excellence is Bhagat Singh. His legacy goes beyond bravery. He showed that success isn't just about physical strength—it's about intelligence, emotional depth, and strong values.

At just 23, Bhagat Singh showed many qualities of a great leader. When he threw a non-lethal bomb in the Central Legislative Assembly, it was a strategic move. He challenged unjust laws without hurting anyone, demonstrating intelligence, strong ethics, and emotional control.

Even in prison, Bhagat Singh showed incredible resilience. He didn't fall into despair. Instead, he spent time writing and thinking, growing intellectually. His hunger strike, which lasted over 100 days, showed not just physical strength but also emotional endurance and empathy for others.

What set Bhagat Singh apart was his deep commitment to the cause of freedom. His strong beliefs gave him the courage to face death with a smile, turning his sacrifice into a symbol of hope for the nation.

Conclusion: Holistic Excellence for a Better Future

Bhagat Singh's life is a perfect example of how intellectual, emotional, and social strengths come together to create true excellence. Just as in competitive exams and in nature, success in life comes from being adaptable and well-rounded.

By promoting this idea of holistic development in education, work, and society, we can create a future where everyone has the opportunity to grow, adapt, and succeed in their own unique way.

The Power of Selflessness: Lessons from History and Business

That wise saying highlights the importance of learning from others' experiences to avoid similar pitfalls. By discussing Mindset 13, I am providing valuable insights to help Mindset 3 individuals recognize potential bad habits and stay cautious.

This approach aligns with the concept of "vicarious learning," where individuals learn from others' experiences, successes, and failures. By sharing knowledge and experiences, you're facilitating a safer and more efficient learning process.

Introduction: The Two Mindsets

Throughout history, success has often been driven by two opposing approaches: selflessness (Mindset 3) and selfishness (Mindset 13). Selflessness is about helping others, building trust, and creating lasting value. Selfishness, on the other hand, emphasizes short-term gains, often ignoring long-term consequences. Whether in leadership or business, examples abound to show that selflessness fosters enduring success, while selfishness leads to eventual failure.

This chapter explores how the principles of selflessness and selfishness have shaped organizations, leaders, and historical movements, offering actionable lessons for the modern world.

The Influence of Consumers and Corporate Decisions

Why Companies Target Human Desires

Modern companies are masters at understanding and influencing human behavior. They recognize that people strive to control their impulses and reduce unnecessary consumption, so they craft strategies to override these instincts. By appealing to emotions rather than needs, businesses often prioritize immediate gratification over sustainable value.

Example: Social media platforms deploy algorithms to capture and retain attention, often at the expense of users' mental health. These platforms rely on an engagement-driven business model, keeping people scrolling for hours to maximize profits.

Outcome: While these strategies yield short-term success, they risk eroding trust, damaging reputation, and ultimately losing user loyalty.

The Declining Lifespan of Companies

The average lifespan of Fortune 500 companies has fallen dramatically, with many now lasting less than 25 years. A primary reason is their focus on short-term financial results at the cost of customer satisfaction and ethical practices.

- Companies that fail to adapt to changing consumer expectations or neglect the long-term repercussions of their strategies often face rapid declines.

Lesson: A fixation on immediate gains may deliver quick wins but leads to unsustainable outcomes.

Mindset 13: The Cost of Selfish Choices

Selfishness may provide short-term victories, but it often leads to personal dissatisfaction and systemic collapse.

Key Traits of Mindset 13

Driven by Greed: A relentless pursuit of wealth or power, often ignoring the well-being of others. Addictions and Vices: Common indulgences include substance abuse, jealousy, or harmful habits, reflecting inner instability. Ego and Competition: Constant comparison and rivalry create toxic environments, breaking trust and relationships. Superficial Success: Outward achievements often hide a lack of true happiness and fulfillment.

Example of Selfishness Leading to Failure :

The Fall of the Roman Empire: Despite its strength, the Roman Empire crumbled under the weight of selfish leadership. Leaders prioritized personal wealth and power over the well-being of their citizens, weakening the system from within.

Mindset 3: The Strength of Selfless Leadership

In contrast, selflessness fosters trust, resilience, and sustainable growth. Individuals and organizations that embrace this mindset leave behind legacies of positive impact.

Key Traits of Mindset 3

Focus on Others: Selfless leaders prioritize the well-being of their team, customers, and society. Balanced Living: They avoid toxic behaviors, instead seeking harmony with people and nature. Strong Relationships: Built on trust and respect, these connections last for generations. Inner Fulfillment: By creating value for others, they find deeper purpose and satisfaction in life.

Leaders Who Embody Selflessness

Great leaders often put the interests of their people above their own, inspiring trust and loyalty:

- **Mahatma Gandhi & Nelson Mandela:** covered in earlier chapters as global examples .

- **Abraham Lincoln:** His leadership during the American Civil War was marked by a focus on preserving the Union and abolishing slavery, despite immense personal and political challenges.

Lesson: Selfless leadership creates legacies that endure far beyond the individual.

The Power of Selflessness

Companies That Thrive on Selflessness

In contrast to short-lived organizations, some companies have built legacies by prioritizing long-term value and ethical practices:

- **Toyota:** Toyota's commitment to quality and continuous improvement has established it as a trusted brand worldwide.

- **Tata Group:** With its focus on community welfare and ethical practices, Tata has cultivated a loyal customer base that spans generations.

- **Sony:** By investing in innovation and customer satisfaction, Sony has remained a leader in the competitive tech and entertainment sectors.

> **❝**
>
> *Selfishness to selflessness: a transformative path where love, purpose, and fulfillment unfold, yielding a life of priceless richness.*
>
> **❞**
>
> — *Rajeev Kharyal*

Section-D
Summary
(Chapters 16-20)

IQ, EQ, and SQ: These three types of intelligence are deeply connected and important for both personal and professional success. But it's important to approach this knowledge with humility, not arrogance. When IQ, EQ, and SQ work together, they create balanced leadership, better teamwork, and help people adapt to our changing world.

The Challenge of Change: Even with all the information available, many people find it hard to make real changes in their lives. This is because our minds are often cluttered with too many thoughts. A balanced mind helps us manage these distractions.

The 'Monkey Mind': This term describes a restless mind that constantly jumps from one thought to another, making it hard to focus and make decisions. This can cause stress and reduce productivity. However, with mindfulness and mental discipline, we can train our minds to stay focused and calm.

Managing Thoughts: Learning to manage your thoughts is a key skill. Thoughts can be helpful (like solving problems) or harmful (like causing burnout). By focusing on important thoughts and letting go of unnecessary ones, we can think clearly and act with purpose.

Virtues Wellness Scale: This tool helps individuals measure their focus and improve their thought management. It helps people assess how well they are managing their thoughts and offers ways to improve their focus, which leads to better mental clarity.

Focus and Thought Relationship: The fewer thoughts we have, the more energy we can devote to each one. Like focusing light on a single point, focused thoughts have the power to overcome obstacles. By reducing unnecessary thoughts, individuals can improve their focus and concentration.

Holistic Excellence: Success in life requires more than just knowledge; it also needs leadership, problem-solving, and emotional intelligence. This idea applies to competitive exams like IAS or MBA programs and in all areas of life.

Excellence in All Areas: Whether in sports, arts, relationships, or work, success comes from a mix of intellectual, emotional, and practical skills. It's important for schools, workplaces, and families to encourage this well-rounded development.

A Better Future: The goal is to create a world where everyone can develop their unique strengths and contribute meaningfully to society. By fostering holistic development, we can face the challenges of life with confidence and resilience, leading to a brighter future for everyone.

Chapter 21

Moving Towards a Goal

How IQ, EQ, and SQ Work Together

Each of these intelligences—IQ, EQ, and SQ—builds on the other, creating a more complete picture of human development. While IQ helps us think critically and achieve personal success, EQ allows us to connect with others and foster meaningful relationships. SQ, finally, encourages us to think beyond our own interests, focusing on making a positive impact on society.

Together, these three intelligences form a powerful framework for navigating life's complexities, from personal achievement to leading others and contributing to society at large.

The Role of Each Quotient at Different Levels

As we progress through different stages of our careers and lives, IQ, EQ, and SQ play distinct roles. Here's how each quotient contributes to leadership and personal development:

IQ at the Executive Level

In executive roles, IQ plays a significant role. Critical thinking, analytical problem-solving, and strategic decision-making are crucial for personal and organizational success. Executives who leverage their intellectual capacity excel in navigating complex challenges, making them invaluable at this level. However, IQ-driven performance has its limitations if not supplemented with EQ and SQ.

EQ at the Managerial Level

As individuals move into managerial positions, EQ becomes more prominent. Managers must build relationships, inspire teams, and navigate interpersonal dynamics. Emotional intelligence, including empathy, self-awareness, and emotional regulation, is key to creating a cohesive, productive work environment. At this level, a strong EQ allows managers to motivate their teams, resolve conflicts, and foster collaboration—skills critical for effective leadership.

SQ at the Leadership Level

At the highest levels of leadership, SQ—which involves moral and ethical decision-making, social responsibility, and a focus on collective well-being—becomes the most important intelligence. True leaders transcend personal and organizational goals, aiming to make a positive impact on society. The ability to lead with purpose and integrity, considering the greater good, defines the top 3% of leaders in any field.

Inner Victory

> **Few, with the wisdom to balance both Social and Spiritual Quotients — two sides of the same coin — have truly conquered life, not for the world to see, but for the view within.**
>
> *— Rajeev Kharyal*

Achieving Balance Between IQ, EQ, and SQ

Executives who aspire to reach the top echelons of leadership must cultivate all three intelligences—IQ, EQ, and SQ—at the right time. While IQ may be sufficient for success in early career stages, progression to higher leadership roles, especially into the top 3%, requires a deep understanding and application of both EQ and SQ.

Delaying the development of EQ and SQ can hinder leadership growth, making it difficult for executives to transition from managerial positions to true leadership. Without EQ, they may struggle to inspire and retain their teams; without SQ, they may fail to make the ethical, impactful decisions necessary to lead in a way that benefits both their organization and society as a whole.

By developing all three intelligences, leaders can balance personal achievement with collective well-being, enabling them to make a lasting positive impact. As the old saying goes, "A stitch in time saves nine"— taking early action to develop EQ for managerial success and SQ for higher leadership can prevent greater challenges down the road

Human Excellence is the journey from

Right ➤ More Right ➤ Absolute Right

From Doers to Holistic Achieverss: Levels of Leadership Growth

Most people, known as "Doers" (about 84% of us), focus on routines and tasks, using IQ to solve problems at work. But without developing EQ and SQ, their potential remains limited. To grow, Doers must begin questioning the world and exploring deeper connections with themselves and others.

Thinkers (13%): These individuals go beyond just using IQ. They develop EQ by exploring their emotions and improving relationships. Thinkers grow by questioning long-held beliefs and embracing personal development.

Holistic Achieverss (3%): These are those individuals who have developed IQ, EQ, and SQ. They understand how society works and are driven by a desire to make a positive impact. They combine intelligence, emotional awareness, and social responsibility into a life filled with meaning and purpose.

Mastering all three intelligences allows these individuals to reach their full potential, becoming leaders who inspire change on both a personal and societal level.

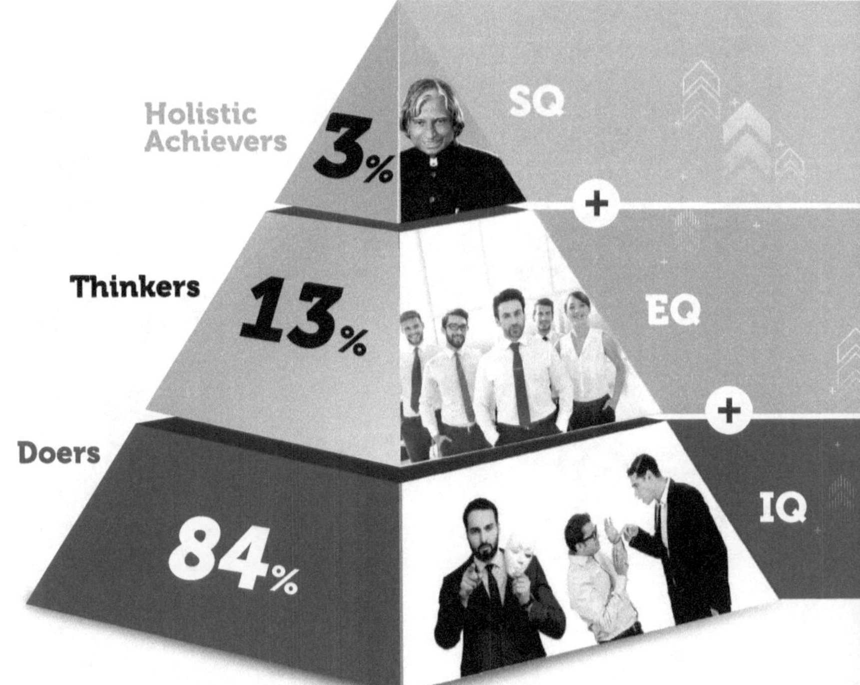

Understanding Moral Complexity

In the pursuit of mastery over IQ, EQ, and SQ, leaders must also navigate the complex moral landscape of real-world decision-making. Life rarely offers clear-cut choices between right and wrong. Instead, it presents shades of grey, where intent, motivation, and context influence the moral implications of our actions.

The ability to understand this complexity is rooted in SQ, where ethical decision-making takes center stage. Consider how intent is weighed in our judicial system—a life taken in self-defense is viewed differently than one taken for personal gain. Leaders must recognize that moral dilemmas require more than just intellectual solutions; they demand empathy, integrity, and social responsibility

> *The Indian judicial system places significant emphasis on the intent behind an act, especially in cases of human loss, to ensure justice is fair and balanced. For example, actions taken by law enforcement officers in good faith while performing their duties may be judged leniently or even recognized if they result in unavoidable loss of life. Conversely, acts driven by harmful motives, such as greed or deliberate harm, typically result in stricter punishments, with the severity aligned to the seriousness of the intent. In evaluating such cases, we have outlined seven categories of human loss (ranging from -3 to +3), where the degree of punishment or reward is determined by the extent of selflessness or selfishness behind the act. This approach ensures that the judiciary considers both the nature of the action and the intent, promoting fairness while upholding societal values.*

The Power of Intent: Shaping Actions and Outcomes

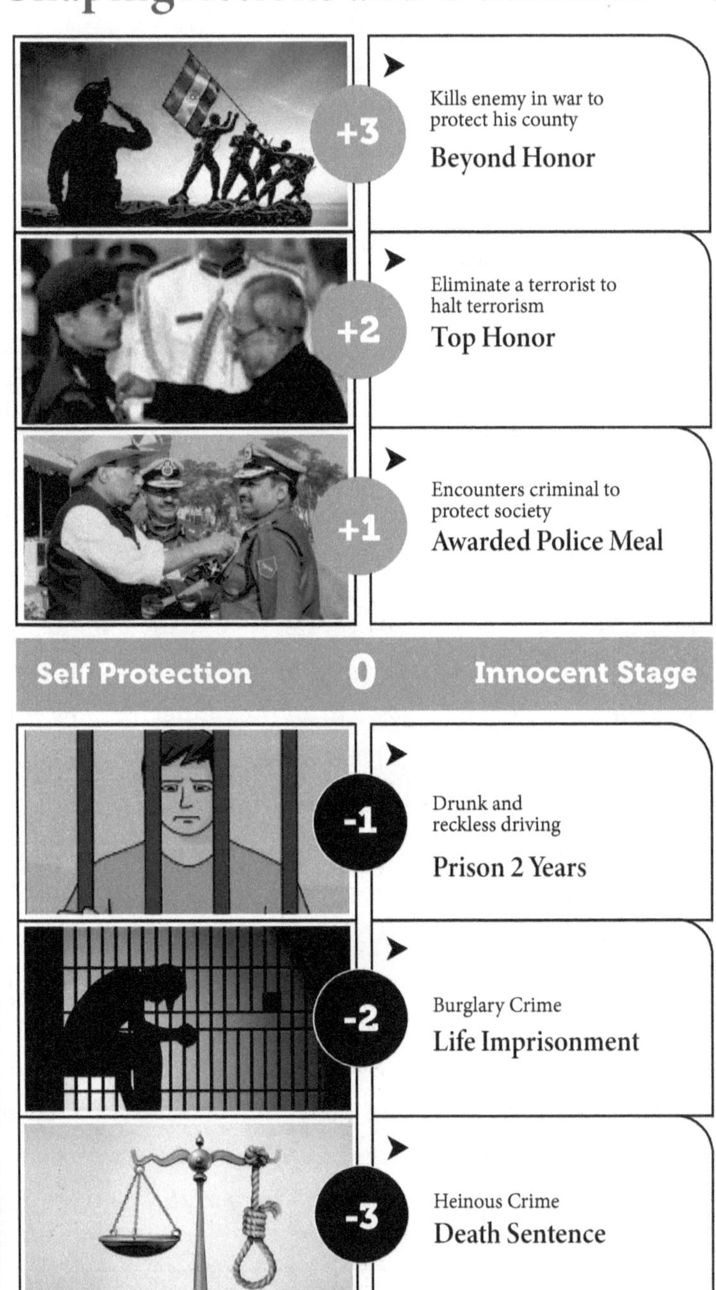

A Lesson from The Good Place

+2 Donating without name and fame

+1 Donating when someone asks to do it

-1 Donating for name and fame

-2 Donating for getting done personal or business work

Intentions Matter: A Lesson from The Good Place

A good example of how intentions affect outcomes can be seen in the show The Good Place. In the show, four people end up in the Bad Place—hell—after they die. One of the characters, Tahani Al-Jamil, is a wealthy philanthropist who raised money for charities and did good deeds on Earth. However, she still finds herself in the Bad Place.

As the story unfolds, we learn that Tahani's real reason for organizing these charity events wasn't true kindness. Instead, she wanted to show off and prove she was better than her sister. Later, after her journey of self-discovery, she writes a book called Get Out of the Spotlight, but ironically, this puts her back in the spotlight!

Tahani's character reflects the reality for many of us. Our actions are often not purely right or wrong, but a mix of choices we make in the moment. Where our actions fall on the scale of right or wrong depends on our intentions and self-awareness.

Achieving Balance: Why It Matters

To live a fulfilling life, we must balance IQ, EQ, and SQ. Relying only on IQ might lead to individual success, but without EQ, relationships suffer, and without SQ, we lack a sense of purpose. Combining all three is essential for true leadership and fulfillment.

The journey from "I" (IQ) to "We" (EQ) to "Our" (SQ) reflects personal growth and collective excellence. When our actions align with the well-being of society, we contribute not only to our own success but also to a better world.

The world around us reflects not only our strengths but also the aspects of ourselves we may overlook—like fears or habits that influence our decisions. Recognizing these challenges isn't about blaming ourselves but about gaining the power to change and move toward a more positive, empowered state.

Instead of viewing our flaws or vices as enemies, we can see them as opportunities to better understand our deeper needs. For example, fear might signal insecurity or disconnection. By addressing these feelings, we can transform vices into virtues. Jealousy, for instance, can shift into love when we focus on finding meaning and fulfillment in our lives.

To support this journey of self-discovery, I've developed this personal growth scale. It's not meant to judge but to help us understand our relationship to both virtues and vices. Self-awareness is a lifelong process that requires courage, honesty, and a willingness to embrace who we truly are. It involves recognizing the positive (virtues) and negative (vices) energies we carry within.

By becoming aware of these influences, we can gradually shift from a self-centered focus to a shared, and ultimately societal, focus. This reflection guide encourages you to rate your emotional awareness: virtues (positive qualities) score between 0 and +3, while vices (negative habits) score between -3 and 0. Your total score serves as a measure of your personal growth and alignment with society.

As you work on enhancing your good traits and transforming your negative ones, your outlook on life changes. You begin to better understand the actions and feelings of others, which naturally leads to more meaningful relationships and effective collaboration with those who share your values. Over time, your environment will reflect the personal growth you've achieved.

The energy you put into the world will return to you. When you spread kindness and positivity, you attract similar experiences. While life may present challenges, each time you choose to stay positive, even in difficult times, you move closer to the life you desire

Chapter 22

The Power of Conscious Choice

The Power of Conscious Choice

Do we choose to stay as passive observers in our own lives, going along with whatever happens and meeting society's expectations? Or do we take control of our destiny and begin a journey of self-discovery and personal growth?

Being in the middle sections of the The Virtues Wellness Scale (13 and 84) isn't necessarily wrong, but staying there can prevent you from reaching your full potential. This scale, as discussed earlier, represents different levels of personal growth, with the majority of people staying at mid-levels, where they often focus on self-interest or routine. However, only by making conscious choices and taking deliberate action can we overcome our limitations, achieve real personal excellence, and reach the highest level (segment 3), where personal success and societal good align.

The First Step: Wanting More

Swami Vivekananda once said,

> **66**
> *Take up one idea. Make that one idea your life—think of it, dream of it, live on that idea... This is the way to success.*
> **99**

Reflecting on my corporate career, I remember a young executive I once mentored. She came to me frustrated and said, "Rajeev, I feel like I'm just going through the motions. Is this all there is?" Her question expressed something many people feel—a deep desire for more meaning in life.

This desire for something more is the first step toward change. It's your inner self telling you to step out of your comfort zone and explore your full potential. But how do we move from simply feeling this desire to taking concrete action?

My Transformational Journey: From Success to Significance

Reflecting on my own two-decade leadership journey, I've traversed the spectrum from Doer to Thinker and finally, to Holistic Achiever. Through a journey of trials and triumphs and moving up and down on snakes and ladders due to tussle between virtues and vices besides many other factors learnt during experiences as detailed throughout the book in my professional and personal journey , I've come to realize the transformative power of embracing Truth, Faith, and Gratitude. At the peak of my corporate success, I felt unfulfilled, drained, and joyless. This turning point sparked a conscious choice to redefine my path. I explored mindfulness, self-reflection, and developed my social quotient (SQ), connecting with something greater than myself and uncovering new meaning and purpose.

By integrating Truth, Faith, and Gratitude into my leadership approach, I've unlocked my full potential, joining the Top 3% League of Holistic Achievers. This journey requires resilience and determination, as one must be willing to pay the price of both personal and professional growth, just as one pays taxes on their hard-earned income. Through this journey, I've learned that conscious choices become the critical success factor throughout this journey.

As I reflect on my two-decade

leadership journey, I'm grateful for the opportunity to inspire and mentor junior colleagues. Many have adopted the '03 mindset,' embracing humility, empathy, and long-term success. This approach has yielded remarkable results: sustained success, positive impact, and a legacy of growth. In contrast, the '13 mindset' often prioritizes short-term gains, leading to burnout and regret.

I'm thrilled to share that my '03 mindset' diversified tools have been well-received by leaders and delegates at national and international workshops and seminars, where I've incorporated them into my professional presentations. The encouraging feedback validates the impact of these practical tools in empowering leaders to adopt a more sustainable and effective approach.

As we embark on this transformational journey, it's essential to recognize that the path ahead won't be straightforward. It's more like a winding road, full of unexpected twists, steep climbs, and some downhill moments. But it's these challenges that shape who we are and help us realize our full potential.

Just like the elephant tied to a small stake with a thin rope, we often hold ourselves back with limiting beliefs formed early in life. To grow and change, we must recognize these limitations and choose to break free from them. Mindfulness, self-reflection, and conscious decision-making can help us overcome these obstacles and move closer to our goals.

As Rabindranath Tagore said, "Let us not pray to be sheltered from dangers, but to be fearless when facing them." This journey requires courage, persistence, and a willingness to step out of our comfort zone for the sake of personal growth.

> **66**
> *Let us not pray to be sheltered from dangers,*
> *but to be fearless when facing them."*
> **99**
> *– Rabindranath Tagore*

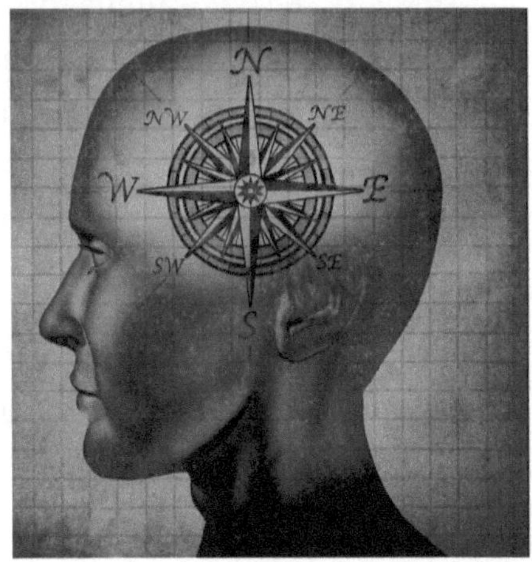

The Compass Analogy: A Simple Guide to Life Choices

Your inner compass guides you in making decisions that align with your values and goals.

Know Your True North: Identify what truly matters to you—your core values and priorities. Stay mindful of pressures, emotions, or biases that could sway your choices.

Plan Your Path: Consider the impact of your decision—both now and in the future—and ensure it feels right. Life evolves, so regularly check if your choices still match your goals.

Quick Check Before Deciding:

Does this align with my values?

Does it feel right?

Will it help me achieve my goals?

Use your inner compass to stay focused and make confident, meaningful choices in every situation.

Set Clear, Purpose-Driven Goals

As Swami Vivekananda said, choose a single goal or idea that drives you. Break that goal down into manageable steps and make choices that bring you closer to it each day. Mindful goal-setting ensures your actions align with your values and long-term aspirations.

Use the Virtues Wellness Scale

Revisit the The Virtues Wellness Scale to assess where you are on your journey. Are your choices driven by self-interest, or are you considering the broader impact on others? The goal is to evolve from focusing solely on "I" (IQ) to "We" (EQ), and eventually "Our" (SQ), where your decisions benefit both you and society.

Seek Feedback and Support

Personal growth doesn't happen in isolation. Seek feedback from trusted mentors, friends, or family. Sometimes, an outside perspective can help reveal areas where you're stuck or where you could improve.

Closing Reflections and a Challenge: Preparing for What's Ahead

As I bring this main part of the book to a close, I want to leave you with one essential thought: personal growth is not about becoming someone else; it's about becoming the best version of yourself. This journey involves embracing your strengths, acknowledging your weaknesses, and committing to continuous improvement. You hold the power to shape your future, break free from limitations, and lift others as you rise.

Before moving forward, I offer you a challenge: identify one "rope" in your life—whether it's a belief, fear, or expectation that's holding you back—and take a small but meaningful step toward freeing yourself from it. Remember, every transformative journey begins with a single step. Face the road ahead with courage, curiosity, and kindness. The path may not always be easy, but it will certainly be rewarding.

The future doesn't merely happen; it's something we create with our choices and actions. So, I ask you: Are you ready to create your future?

Pathway to the Final Chapters
(Chapters 23 to 25)

Now, as we move into the final chapters, you'll find a collection of expanded insights and self-assessment tools designed to support your continued journey. In these upcoming chapters, you'll explore the path from vices to virtues, find balance through mindful alignment, and apply self-assessment tools to measure and guide your personal progress. Each chapter offers strategies that enable you to live more intentionally and join the league of those who experience life with greater purpose, clarity, and fulfillment. Together, these final insights will equip you to carry forward the work you've begun, helping you refine and sustain a path that's truly your own.

Chapter 23

The Journey from Vices to Virtues

Virtue's breath

> **Just as our bodies need oxygen and release carbon dioxide, our souls thrive when we embrace virtues and release vices.**

— *Rajeev Kharyal*

The journey from vices to virtues is a lifelong process of growth, guiding us toward inner peace and stronger, more fulfilling relationships with ourselves and others.

Virtues and Vices Through Life Stages

As we grow, virtues and vices influence us in different ways at each stage of life. Recognizing how they manifest can help us make better choices and live with purpose.

1 Early Life and Adolescence: Building Foundations

- **Family Influence:** Love and compassion build a strong emotional foundation, while jealousy can create insecurity.

- **Peer Pressure:** Honesty and courage are often tested by the desire to fit in.

- **Developing Courage:** Facing new experiences teaches courage, helping balance strengths and fears.

2 Adulthood: Managing Complex Challenges

- **Career and Relationships:** Patience and resilience are essential as adults juggle responsibilities, but fear of failure can challenge honesty.

- **Financial Pressure:** Money concerns may lead to vices like worry or obsession, testing virtues like courage and sound decision-making.

3 Mid-Life: Reflection and Realignment

- **Reevaluating Choices:** This stage involves reflecting on past decisions and assessing whether they were guided by virtues or influenced by vices like ego. Seeking Meaning: Joy, contentment, and humility often become priorities over ambition, leading to greater fulfillment.

4 Old Age: Wisdom and Acceptance

- **Finding Peace:** Gratitude and love grow stronger, while anger and ego tend to fade.

- **Accepting Mortality:** Faith and truth help release fear and doubt, bringing peace in the natural cycle of life.

By understanding how virtues and vices evolve, we can better navigate life's stages, making choices that align with our values and foster a sense of peace and fulfillment.

Exploring the duality of human nature

Virtues and vices exist as opposites, with each virtue countering a corresponding vice. Choosing virtues leads to clarity, purpose, and harmony, while vices create confusion and imbalance. Here's a simple comparison:

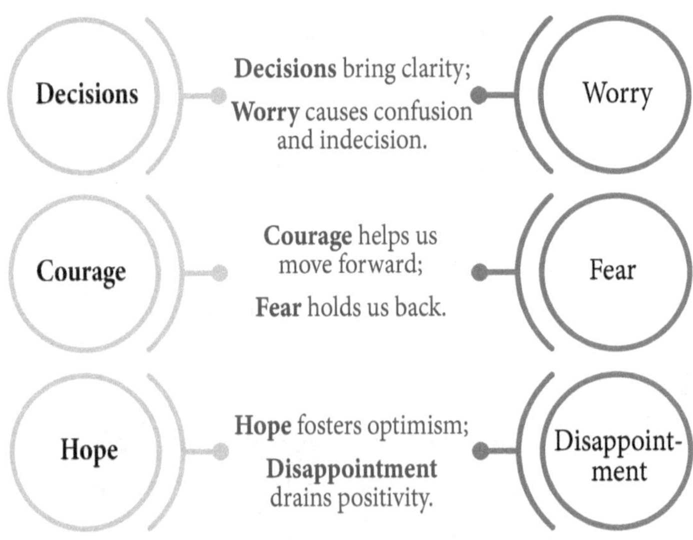

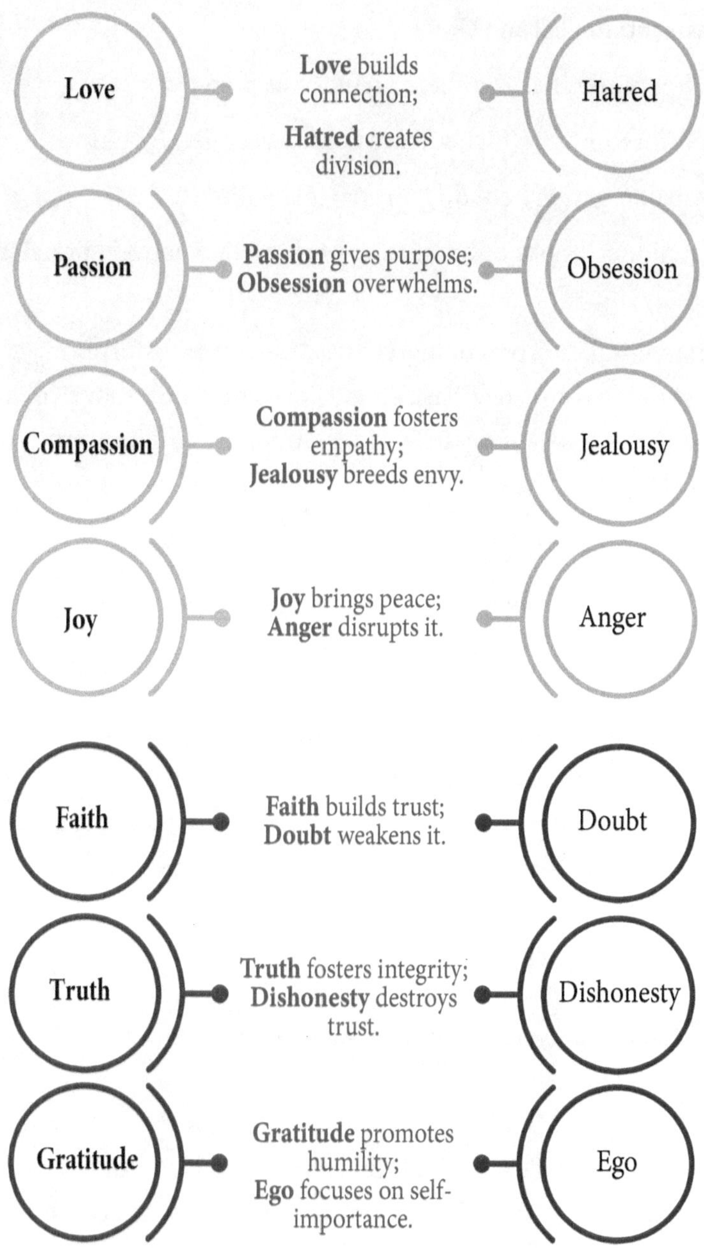

Love
Love builds connection;
Hatred creates division.
Hatred

Passion
Passion gives purpose;
Obsession overwhelms.
Obsession

Compassion
Compassion fosters empathy;
Jealousy breeds envy.
Jealousy

Joy
Joy brings peace;
Anger disrupts it.
Anger

Faith
Faith builds trust;
Doubt weakens it.
Doubt

Truth
Truth fosters integrity;
Dishonesty destroys trust.
Dishonesty

Gratitude
Gratitude promotes humility;
Ego focuses on self-importance.
Ego

Self-Assessment: Reflect and Grow

Take a moment to reflect on these virtue-vice pairs:

Identify Strengths: Which virtues come naturally to you?

Spot Challenges: Where do you struggle with vices?

Take Action: Choose one virtue to work on and actively practice it in your daily life.

By understanding and practicing virtues, we can transform our actions and thoughts. This journey isn't about perfection but about consistent growth. The more we align with virtues, the more fulfilled and peaceful our lives become.

GRASPING THE ESSENCE OF VIRTUES AND VICES

The Nutrients and Toxins of the Mind and Body Virtues act as mental "nutrients," strengthening our minds and bodies, enhancing clarity, and fostering meaningful connections. In contrast, vices function as toxins, clouding our thoughts, adding stress, and disrupting inner peace. Choosing virtues over vices is like opting for nutritious food over junk food—it brings balance, effectiveness, and sustained happiness.

Virtue Nutrient Connection Emotional Benefit Physical Benefit Overall Impact

Gratitude Vitamin C Boosts immunity like gratitude builds resilience. Strengthens positivity. Enhances immune system. Nourishes relationships.Truth Protein Builds structure like truth fosters integrity. Enhances trust and respect. Supports body tissue health. Solidifies trust and stability. Faith Calcium Grounds body like faith grounds emotions. Reduces anxiety. Strengthens bones. Provides emotional stability.

Virtue Nutrient Connection Chart

Virtue	Nutrient	Connection	Emotional Benefit	Physical Benefit	Overall Impact
Gratitude	Vitamin C	Boosts immunity like gratitude builds resilience.	Strengthens positivity.	Enhances immune system.	Nourishes relationships.
Truth	Protein	Builds structure like truth fosters integrity.	Enhances trust and respect.	Supports body tissue health.	Solidifies trust and stability.
Faith	Calcium	Grounds body like faith grounds emotions.	Reduces anxiety.	Strengthens bones.	Provides emotional stability.
Passion	Iron	Energizes body like passion fuels drive.	Fuels motivation.	Boosts energy.	Inspires action and ambition.
Compassion	Magnesium	Soothes stress like compassion eases tension.	Fosters empathy and calm.	Calms nerves.	Builds supportive connections.
Love	Vitamin D	Brings light like love enhances connection.	Deepens bonds.	Improves mood.	Promotes collaboration.
Joy	Endorphins	Lifts mood like joy boosts resilience.	Fosters optimism.	Natural pain relief.	Spreads positivity.
Hope	Antioxidants	Protects cells like hope shields optimism.	Inspires persistence.	Combats stress.	Fuels growth and vitality.
Courage	Potassium	Balances body like courage steadies fears.	Promotes boldness.	Supports heart health.	Enables decisive action.
Decision	Omega-3s	Improves focus and clarity	Boosts brain health	Helps set and achieve meaningful goals	Helps achieve goals.

Vice Toxin Connection Emotional Harm Physical Harm Overall Impact Chart

Vice	Toxin	Connection	Emotional Harm	Physical Harm	Overall Impact
Ego	Saturated Fats	Blocks flow like ego blocks connection.	Isolates and limits connection.	Clogs arteries.	Creates isolation, hinders collaboration.
Dishonesty	Artificial Sweeteners	Appears sweet but causes hidden harm.	Destabilizes trust.	Causes hidden long-term harm.	Diminishes credibility, reduces cooperation.
Doubt	Acidic Foods	Eats away at confidence like acid erodes.	Undermines confidence.	Harms teeth and digestion.	Lowers self-belief, hampers productivity.
Obsession	Processed Sugars	Provides a rush but leads to crashes.	Fosters unhealthy fixations.	Leads to energy crashes.	Distorts balance, disrupts harmony.
Jealousy	Excessive Caffeine	Overstimulates like jealousy unsettles.	Brings restlessness.	Raises heart rate.	Breeds resentment, disturbs harmony.
Hatred	Trans Fats	Hardens emotions like trans fats harden.	Hardens emotions.	Increases heart risks.	Fosters hostility, alienates others.
Anger	Alcohol	Clouds judgment like alcohol does.	Promotes impulsive reactions.	Damages liver, clouds clarity.	Causes conflict, harms reputation.
Dis-appointment	High-Fructose Syrup	Feels sweet but crashes motivation.	Leads to emotional crashes.	Causes energy fluctuations.	Lowers morale and motivation.
Fear	Environmental Toxins	Builds negativity like toxins accumulate.	Instills worry.	Accumulates in the body.	Limits growth, stifles creativity.
Worry	Processed Foods	Lacks nourishment like worry lacks clarity.	Leads to burnout.	Lacks real nourishment.	Drains focus and productivity.

provide deeper and more enduring satisfaction, building a foundation for genuine peace and purpose.

Trust in Institutions: With many feeling disillusioned by institutions—whether governments, corporations, or social systems—there's a growing tendency to question the need for values. Yet, when institutions falter, personal virtues become even more essential. They empower us to build trust, foster stronger relationships, and create resilient communities, no matter the external chaos.

Virtues as Life's Constants: Just as our body depends on steady breathing and a stable heart rate, virtues offer a constant source of stability in a changing world. They connect us to others and strengthen our resilience, acting as timeless guides for a meaningful life, regardless of external pressures.

Fulfillment Through Virtues: People who live by values like honesty, empathy, gratitude, and passion often experience a greater sense of well-being and purpose. While vices may offer convenience, they can't replace the lasting peace that comes from a life built on values. True happiness isn't found in shortcuts but in the steady fulfillment that virtues bring.

Though some may promote a "new normal" where values seem less important, virtues remain timeless and universal, unaffected by wealth, background, or status. In a world of constant change, virtues are essential for true happiness and resilience, offering a path to lasting contentment that shortcuts simply can't match.

Moving Forward

Choosing virtues over vices enriches both our inner world and our relationships, helping us create a life of resilience, clarity, and positive impact. By understanding how virtues and vices influence us, we can make intentional choices that lead to a balanced and purposeful life.

As we continue, let's explore how finding balance and self-assessment can further support this journey toward fulfillment and well-being.

Chapter 24

Finding Balance

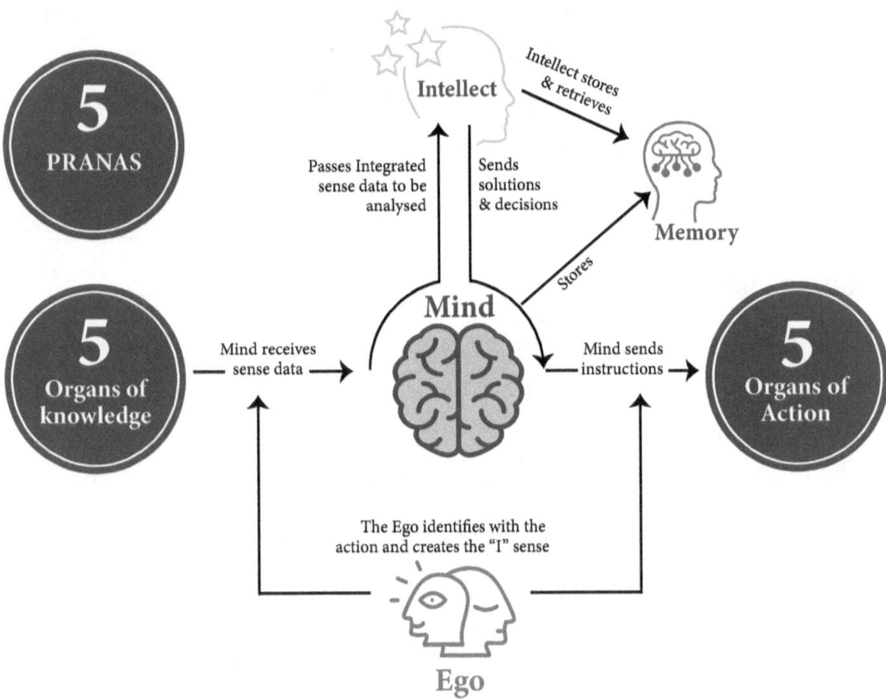

Subtle body illustration

The Chakra Virtues & Vices Matrix

Chakras are energy centers in our bodies that, when balanced, contribute to our physical and emotional health. Each chakra embodies specific virtues (positive qualities) and vices (negative traits). When balanced, these chakras help us feel grounded, confident, and connected. However, imbalance in a chakra can lead to issues like anxiety, low self-esteem, or even physical discomfort.

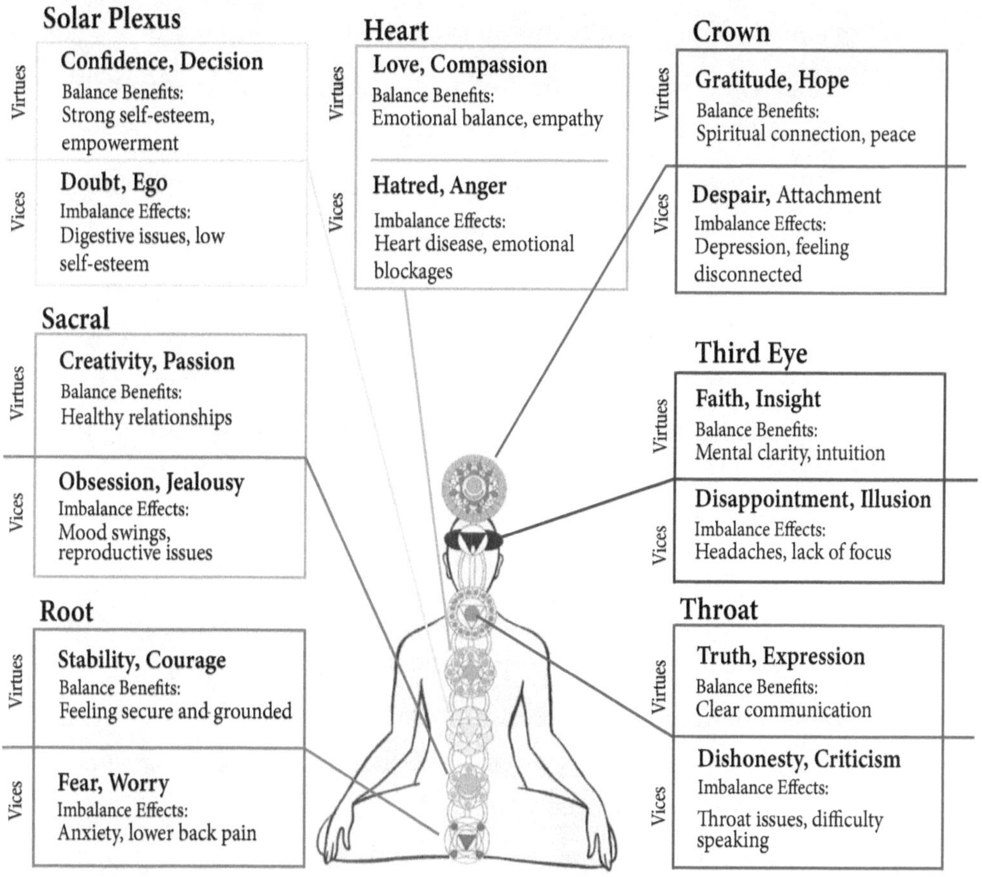

Takeaway: Each chakra holds both virtues and vices. When virtues are strong, we experience balance and inner peace; when vices dominate, we may face emotional or physical discomfort.

The Big Four for Well-Being: The Tree of a Balanced Life

Think of your well-being as a strong, healthy tree. Just like any tree, it needs different parts to stay balanced, grow, and thrive. Four natural chemicals in our bodies — dopamine, serotonin, oxytocin, and endorphins — are like the essential parts of this tree. Each one plays a special role in keeping us motivated, calm, connected, and resilient.

Let's look at how each part of this "Tree of Well-Being" works:

1. Dopamine – The Roots: Motivation and Drive

Dopamine is like the roots of the tree. Roots dig deep and absorb nutrients from the soil, helping the tree grow strong.

- **What Dopamine Does:** Just as roots pull in nutrients, dopamine helps us reach our goals, giving us the drive to try new things and feel rewarded when we succeed.

- **Why It Matters:** Without dopamine, we might feel unmotivated or stuck, like a tree with weak roots.

Roots (Dopamine) keep us grounded and excited to grow, pushing us to achieve.

2. Serotonin – The Trunk: Stability and Calm

Serotonin is like the trunk of the tree. The trunk is strong and stable, supporting the branches and keeping the tree upright.

- **What Serotonin Does:** Like the trunk that holds the tree steady, serotonin helps keep our mood balanced. It gives us a sense of calm and keeps us feeling steady, even on tough days.

- **Why It Matters:** Without enough serotonin, we might feel anxious or unstable, like a tree that can't stand tall.

Trunk (Serotonin) gives us stability and peace, helping us stay grounded.

3. Oxytocin – The Branches: Connection and Bonding

Oxytocin is like the branches of the tree. Branches reach outward, connecting the tree to sunlight, air, and sometimes even nearby trees.

- **What Oxytocin Does:** Just as branches extend and connect the tree to its surroundings, oxytocin helps us connect with others, building trust and friendships.
- **Why It Matters:** Without oxytocin, we might feel lonely or disconnected, like a tree without branches.

Branches (Oxytocin) help us connect with others, forming close bonds and friendships.

4. Endorphins – The Leaves: Resilience and Energy

Endorphins are like the leaves of the tree. Leaves soak up sunlight and turn it into energy, giving the tree life and resilience.

- **What Endorphins Do:** Like leaves that absorb sunlight, endorphins give us energy and help us handle stress or pain. They make us feel strong and positive, especially during challenging times.
- **Why It Matters:** Without endorphins, we might feel worn down and unable to cope with stress, like a tree without healthy leaves.

Leaves (Endorphins) keep us energized and resilient, helping us handle life's ups and downs.

So, next time you're feeling inspired, calm, connected, or resilient, remember it's your inner "Tree of Well-Being" at work, keeping you healthy and happy!

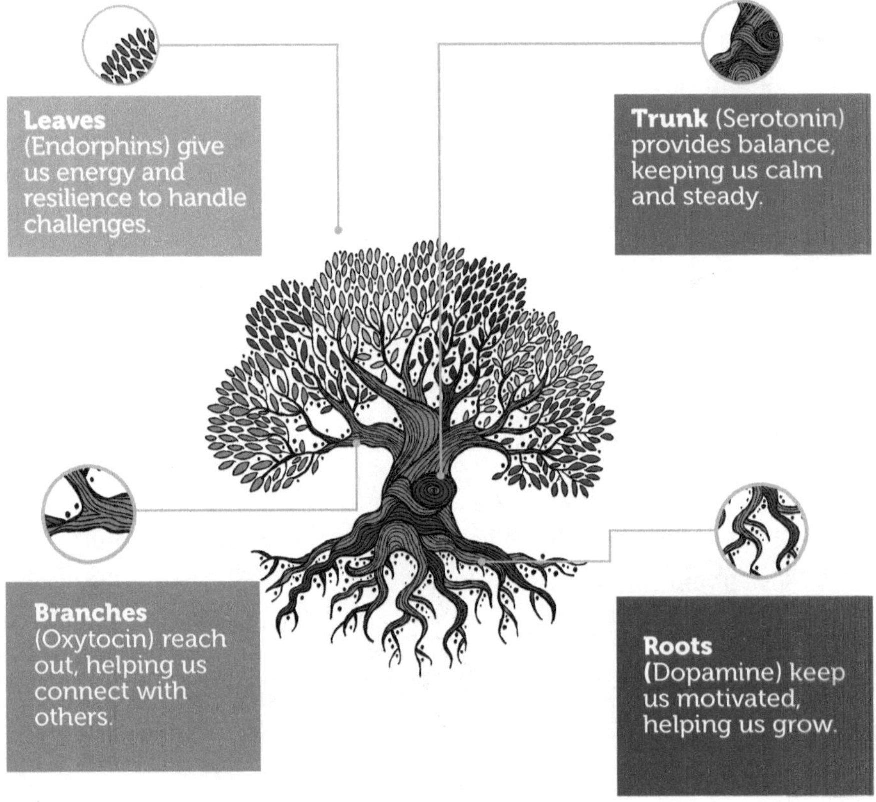

Beyond the Top 3% League: Universal Excellence

Achieving the pinnacle of human excellence requires transcending the gravitational forces holding you back.

**Stage 1: Human Excellence; Overcoming the World's Illusion
(from selfishness to selflessness Intent)**

Like an airplane soaring above the clouds, overcoming earth's gravity, human excellence reaches new heights by:

- Shifting from selfish intent to selfless intent

- Letting go of ego, desires, and attachments

- Embracing empathy, compassion, and service to others

**Stage 2: Universal Excellence; Attaining Egolessness
(from Selflessness to Egolessness Intent)**

Just as a rocket breaks free from earth's gravity, entering orbit, human excellence touches the upper crest by:

- Transcending selfless intent to Egolessness

- Surrendering individuality to universal consciousness

- Embodying purity, clarity, and inner peace

In this elevated state:

- Mind free from ego and desires
- Connection to universal energy fuels pure thoughts and actions
- Individual becomes a magnet, attracting positivity and harmony

The Egolessness State:

- No boundaries, no separation
- Unity with the universe
- Pure awareness, untainted by ego or desires

Key Principles:

- Self-awareness and introspection
- Emotional intelligence and resilience
- Mindfulness and meditation
- Service to others and selflessness
- Surrender and letting go

The Synchronous Generator Analogy:
Imagine two generators, regardless of capacity, synchronizing parameters (voltage, frequency, etc.) to serve a unified load. Similarly, universal excellence requires harmonizing individual energy with the universe.

Synchronization Parameters:

- **Voltage:** Inner peace and calm
- **Frequency:** Vibrational alignment with universal energy
- **Phase:** Unity and coherence with the cosmos

Interpreting **Swami Satyanand Ji Maharaj** message from Gita
on moving up from metaphor from airplane to Rocket to cross gravity
aiming to reach and then move free in the orbit thereafter.

This can be attained as Universal Excellence by practising the daily
chores aiming to free from illusion and attain the reunion with divine in
life time itself :

Connect the Higher Conscious Daily

Connecting with our higher conscious daily helps us access guidance,
wisdom, and strength. Take time to quiet the mind, listen to your inner
voice, and align yourself with your true nature.

See Divinity All Around

See the divine in every person, creature, and element. This mindset shift
cultivates reverence, gratitude, and compassion. Live in harmony with
nature and respect the inherent worth of all beings.

Have Enough Surrender

Surrender your ego, biases, and preconceptions to see the truth.
Humility and openness create space for new insights and wisdom to
emerge.

Detach from Illusion, Attach to Reality

Let go of attachment to fleeting pleasures and material possessions. Focus
on cultivating a deep connection with the eternal and unchanging reality.

Prioritize the Divine

Recognize that spiritual growth and connection with the divine are
essential to your well-being and happiness. Prioritize your spiritual
journey and cultivate wisdom, compassion, and strength.

Let's Go!

Embark on a journey of self-discovery, spiritual growth, and service to
others. Take the first step, and then the next, and continue on the path
to your highest potential.

Section-E
Summary
(Chapters 21-25)

Moving Towards a Goal

This chapter introduces the importance of combining intellectual (IQ), emotional (EQ), and social intelligence (SQ) to achieve personal and professional growth. It likens IQ to a compass, EQ to a map, and SQ to the wind that propels us, illustrating how each intelligence complements the other. Together, these elements create a framework for navigating life's complexities, helping individuals reach their goals and make meaningful contributions to the world around them.

The Power of Conscious Choice

Focusing on the power of intentional decision-making, this chapter encourages readers to step out of passive roles in life and make conscious choices that align with personal growth. It emphasizes the importance of self-awareness and inner motivation as the foundation for change, using relatable anecdotes to illustrate how conscious choices can unlock higher levels of fulfillment, personal excellence, and a balanced, purpose-driven life.

The Journey from Vices to Virtues

This chapter explores the transformative journey of turning personal vices into virtues, comparing virtues to mental and physical nutrients and vices to toxins. By identifying and addressing negative traits, individuals can cultivate qualities like courage, hope, and love that enhance well-being and relationships. The chapter highlights how developing virtues over vices contributes to emotional balance, resilience, and a healthier, more connected life.

Finding Balance

Using the concept of chakras, this chapter discusses how aligning positive traits, or virtues, with our core energy centers promotes harmony in mind and body. Each chakra is associated with specific virtues and vices, suggesting that balance in these areas can lead to greater mental clarity, physical health, and emotional well-being. This holistic approach encourages readers to view personal growth as interconnected, emphasizing the benefits of balanced energy for a fulfilling life.

Assess Yourself

The final chapter provides practical self-assessment tools, such as the Virtues Wellness Scale and Intent Scale, to help readers gauge their progress in personal development. Each scale covers aspects like decision-making, emotional control, and intention-setting, offering actionable steps to improve. This chapter empowers readers to track their growth, set meaningful goals, and continually refine their path toward a balanced, purposeful life.

Assess Yourself

In this chapter, we introduce five key self-assessment tools designed to guide you on your journey of personal growth and self-discovery. Each of these scales offers a unique perspective, helping you understand and refine different areas of your life to achieve balance, clarity, and purpose.

5 self-assessment tools

1st The Virtues Wellness Scale assesses the balance between virtues and vices, highlighting areas where qualities like courage and gratitude can be strengthened.

2nd The Guna Harmony Scale evaluates your personality traits and energies, offering insights into achieving inner harmony.

3rd The Intention Impact Scale assesses the quality and influence of your intentions, guiding you from self-centered to enlightened interactions and fostering more positive relationships.

4th The Time Balance Scale examines where your attention is directed—past, present, or future—encouraging you to stay grounded in the present.

5th The Thought Focus Scale measures the clarity and alignment of your thoughts, supporting a purposeful, goal-oriented mindset.

By using these scales, individuals can create a tailored action plan that propels them forward—from the broader 84% group, through the focused 13%, and ultimately into the top 3% league of individuals who live with clarity, purpose, and influence. Remarkably, reaching this top 3% level requires less energy than remaining in the 84% or 13% groups, as it aligns with our natural state of balance and fulfillment.

Once this state is achieved, individuals find themselves effortlessly aligned with the fundamental purpose of life, where growth and contribution feel as natural as breathing. Regular reflection and application of these insights will allow each step to be intentional, aligned, and impactful, accelerating your journey toward your highest potential.

Intellectual Quotient (IQ)
Section

To assess yourself, rate each virtue and vice listed in the table below according to the provided scoring ranges for IQ. This will help you identify your strengths and the areas for improvement.

From Darkness to Enlightenment

> **"**
>
> *Virtues elevate human beings to heavenly realms, while vices descend to hell. Through the transformative power of divine love, the journey from selflessness to egolessness yields true liberation – a profound state of freedom, unity, and inner peace.*
>
> **"**

-Rajeev Kharyal

Decision (vs) Worry

Score	Description	Tips
0	Feeling stuck and overwhelmed by worry.	Start with small, low-risk choices to build confidence.
1	Aware but hesitant; doubts linger.	Write pros and cons to clear up anxiety.
2	Gaining confidence in making decisions.	Look back at good decisions for encouragement.
3	Decisive and clear; trusts own judgment.	Keep trusting yourself based on past success.

Courage (vs) Fear

Score	Description	Tips
0	Overcome by fear; avoids challenges.	Face small fears daily, like speaking up.
1	Recognizes fear and takes small steps.	Picture positive outcomes to build courage.
2	Confronts fear in safe settings; feels braver.	Use mindfulness to stay grounded.
3	Acts with courage; fear no longer holds back.	Step outside your comfort zone to grow further.

Hope (vs) Disappointment

Score	Description	Tips
0	Feeling hopeless; disappointment dominates.	Start with small, achievable goals to rebuild hope.
1	Aware of disappointment, but hopeful glimpses.	Celebrate small wins to sustain momentum.
2	Radiating hope; disappointment no longer defines.	Share hope with others to amplify positivity.
3	Decisive and clear; trusts own judgment	Keep trusting yourself based on past success

The marks be posted on Virtues Wellness Scale placed at page 184-185 in book.

Emotional Quotient (EQ) Section

To assess yourself, rate each virtue and vice listed in the table below according to the provided scoring ranges for EQ. This will help you identify your strengths and the areas for improvement.

From Greed to Giving

Just as our intent on money shifts from greed to meeting needs to enriching lives, our heart intent transforms from selfishness to selflessness to egolessness, ultimately illuminating the path to true fulfillment.

-Rajeev Kharyal

Joy (vs) Anger

Score	Description	Tips
0	Anger takes over; joy is blocked.	Practice calming methods like deep breathing.
1-2	Aware of anger but it still surfaces often.	Shift focus to things you can control.
3-4	Seeking joy, but anger sometimes disrupts.	Use daily gratitude to increase positivity.
5-6	Mostly joyful; anger is well-managed.	Keep nurturing joy and well-being.

Love (vs) Hatred

Score	Description	Tips
0	Feeling hatred; impacts relationships.	Start forgiving and letting go of grudges.
1-2	Realizes need for love, but negativity lingers.	Do small acts of kindness to shift focus.
3-4	Moving towards love; less resentment.	Spend time with uplifting people.
5-6	Guided by love and compassion.	Practice empathy and deep listening.

Compassion (vs) Jealousy

Score	Description	Tips
0	Consumed by jealousy; compassion lacking.	Recognize and acknowledge feelings.
1-2	1-2 Aware of jealousy, but struggles to empathize.	Practice active listening and understanding.
3-4	3-4 Cultivating compassion; jealousy subsides.	Engage in self-reflection and gratitude.
5-6	Radiating compassion; jealousy no longer dominates.	Share kindness and support with others.

Passion (vs) Obsession

Score	Description	Tips
0	Overcome by obsession; stressed and burnt out.	Set limits to prevent burnout.
1-2	Aware of obsession, but hard to control.	Take breaks and practice mindfulness.
3-4	Balances passion, uses it positively.	Channel passion into creative outlets.
5-6	Passion is purposeful and fulfilling.	Align passion with long-term goals.

The marks be posted on Virtues Wellness Scale placed at page 184-185 in book.

Social Quotient (SQ)
Section

To assess yourself, rate each virtue and vice listed in the table below according to the provided scoring ranges for SQ. This will help you identify your strengths and the areas for improvement.

Balancing the Human Design

> **"**
>
> *Human design is a holistic framework comprising physical, subtle, and causal bodies. This integrated network achieves optimal efficiency when the physical body operates at 98.6°F, the subtle body is balanced, and the causal body is guided by egolessness. In this state, the individual experiences harmony, clarity, and purpose.*
>
> **"**
>
> *-Rajeev Kharyal*

Faith **vs** Doubt

Score	Description	Tips
0	Doubt clouds judgment; little faith.	Affirm your strengths and seek supportive people.
1-3	Aware of need for faith, but doubt persists.	Set small goals to build self-trust.
4-6	Growing faith; doubt appears less often.	Reflect on past successes to strengthen belief.
7-9	Unshakable faith in self and path.	Challenge doubt by focusing on your strengths.

Truth **vs** Dishonesty

Score	Description	Tips
0	Dishonest in actions; disconnected from truth.	Start with small truths to build honesty.
1-3	Aware of dishonesty's harm; hard to be truthful.	Practice honesty in safe situations.
4-6	Striving for truth, with occasional insecurity.	Reflect on how truth builds connections.
7-9	Guided by truth; aligned with personal values.	Practice honesty in all aspects of life.

Gratitude **vs** Ego

Score	Description	Tips
0	Driven by ego; little focus on gratitude.	Reflect daily on what you're grateful for.
1-3	Recognizes gratitude's value but struggles with ego.	Celebrate others' successes and practice humility.
4-6	Balancing gratitude and ego.	Do acts of service to enhance gratitude.
7-9	Fully grateful; ego is minimal.	Continue appreciating the present and others.

The marks be posted on Virtues Wellness Scale placed at page 184-185 in book.

How to Use This Scale

1.Self-Assess: Identify where you stand in each area.

2.Take Action: Use the tips provided to progress from one stage to the next.

3.Reflect and Repeat: Regularly check in to track growth and adjust as needed.

This structure makes readers to pinpoint their current stage, take actionable steps, and regularly revisit their progress on the path to personal growth.

The Virtues Wellness Scale

Which type of mind do you have?

To assess yourself, rate each virtue and vice listed in the table below according to the provided scoring ranges for SQ, EQ, and IQ. This will help you identify your strengths and the areas for improvement.

Example:

	9	6	3	0		
Gratitude	☐	✓	☐	☐	=	6 /9

SQ

Fill any one number

	Virtue	9	6	3	0		Virtue Marks
1	**Gratitude**	☐	☐	☐	☐	=	...... /9
2	**Truth**	☐	☐	☐	☐	=	...... /9
3	**Faith**	☐	☐	☐	☐	=	...... /9
						=	...... /27

EQ

Fill any one number

	Virtue	6	4	2	0		Virtue Marks
4	**Passion**	☐	☐	☐	☐	=	...... /6
5	**Compassion**	☐	☐	☐	☐	=	...... /6
6	**Love**	☐	☐	☐	☐	=	...... /6
7	**Joy**	☐	☐	☐	☐	=	...... /6
						=	...... /24

IQ

Fill any one number

	Virtue	3	2	1	0		Virtue Marks
8	**Hope**	☐	☐	☐	☐	=	...... /3
9	**Courage**	☐	☐	☐	☐	=	...... /3
10	**Decision**	☐	☐	☐	☐	=	...... /3
					Total	=	...... /9

Virtue Total Numbers (SQ+EQ+IQ) ...... **/60**

"Virtues lead to heaven, vices to hell. Selfless acts, driven by divine love, yield true liberation (Moksha)."

Ego	(9-6) = 3 /9

9 (-) Virtue Marks

Vice	Vice Marks	Introspection
Ego	........./9	
Dishonest	........./9	
Doubt	........./9	
	........./27	

6 (-) Virtue Marks

Vice	Vice Marks	Introspection
Obsession	........./6	
Jealous	........./6	
Hatred	........./6	
Anger	........./6	
	........./24	

3 (-) Virtue Marks

Vice	Vice Marks	Introspection
Disappointment	........./3	
Fear	........./3	
Worry	........./3	
	........./9	

Guna Harmony Scale

Understand your personality traits and tendencies, and learn to balance your energies for harmony and well-being.

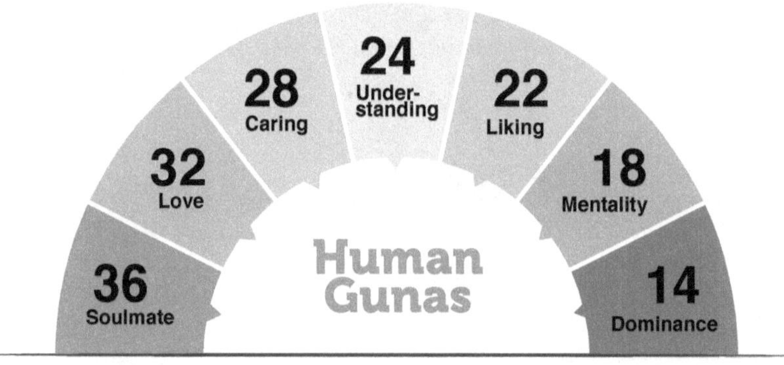

To enhance your relationships with family, friends, and others, consider how many of the 36 qualities or traits (gunas) align with them and **fill in the columns below.**

Core Family Unit

Parents ☐   Spouse ☐   Children ☐

Extended Support Network

Sibling ☐   Friend ☐

Professional Network

Supervisor ☐   Colleague ☐

Levels of Relationships and How to Improve Them

This guide shows different types of relationships, from those with power struggles to deep, soulmate connections, with easy actions to strengthen each one.

Guna 14 | **Dominance**

One person has more control; little empathy

Ways to Improve
- **Listen Actively:** Don't interrupt, show respect.
- **Set Boundaries:** Create fairness.
- **Find Common Goals:** Focus on shared interests to reduce conflict

---

Guna 18 | **Mentality**

Connected on an intellectual level, but not deeply emotional.

Ways to Improve
- **Share Personal Feelings:** Go beyond surface topics.
- **Show Vulnerability:** Open up about experiences.
- **Practice Empathy:** Discuss topics that build emotional closeness.

Guna 22 | **Liking**

Friendly and comfortable, but not deeply connected.

Ways to Improve
- **Spend Quality Time:** Do fun activities together.
- **Express Appreciation:** Share what you like about each other.
- **Build Trust:** Be consistent and reliable.

Guna 24 | **Understanding**

Growing empathy and connection.

Ways to Improve
- **Practice Empathy:** Understand things from their perspective.
- **Ask Open Questions:** Learn about each other's dreams.
- **Celebrate Together:** Enjoy small successes together.

Guna 28 — Caring

Compassionate and nurturing relationship.

Ways to Improve
- **Show Genuine Care:** Support each other's needs.
- **Create Check-Ins:** Make time to connect regularly.
- **Offer Support:** Be there during tough times.

Guna 32 — Love

Deep, holistic connection with care for each other's happiness.

Ways to Improve
- **Support Growth:** Encourage each other's ambitions.
- **Accept Fully:** Embrace strengths and flaws.
- **Express Love Often:** Show love through words and actions.

Guna 36 — Soulmate

Ideal connection with emotional, intellectual, and spiritual unity.

Intention Impact Scale

This scale shows how intentions can range from harmful (red) to enlightened (violet), with each level having a different impact on relationships and interactions.

SELFLESS	NEUTRAL	SELFISH
+1 Supportive Kind and considerate	**0 Balanced** Calm and neutral	**-1 Self-Centered** Detached and indifferent
+2 Compassionate Generous and caring		**-2 Manipulative** Controlling and deceitful
+3 Enlightened Wise and empathetic		**-3 Destructive** Toxic and harmful behavior

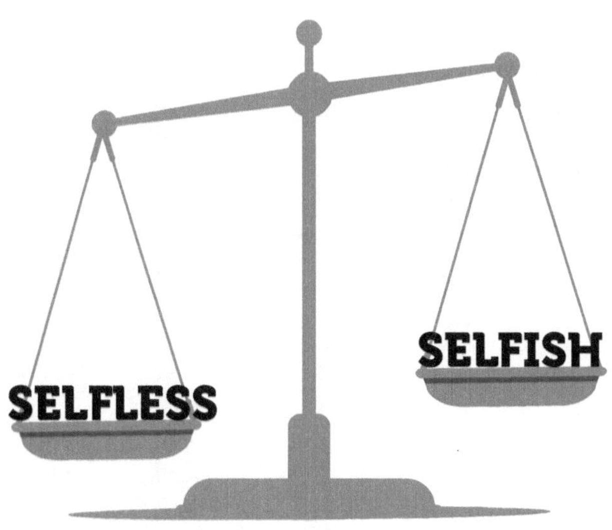

Intent Scale in Relationships

This scale also shows how intentions at each level affect relationships with family, colleagues, and society

Level	Intent	Color	Family	Extended Family	Professional	Society
-3	Destructive	Red	Criticism, verbal abuse	Harmful rumors	Sabotaging work	Spreading misinformation
-2	Manipulative	Orange	Guilt trips	Exclusion, controlling	Taking credit, gossiping	Withholding info
-1	Self-Centered	Yellow	Ignoring others' feelings	Expecting special treatment	Ignoring feedback	Ignoring community needs
0	Balanced	Green	Respecting boundaries	Valuing individuality	Working well together	Supporting social justice
+1	Supportive	Blue	Offering emotional support	Helping when needed	Offering guidance	Volunteering
+2	Compassionate	Indigo	Giving time and support	Donating resources	Supporting coworkers	Advocating for social change
+3	Enlightened	Violet	Unconditional love	Mentoring, promoting harmony	Leading with empathy	Promoting global unity

This scale helps us see how intentions, from negative to positive, affect our interactions. Choosing higher intentions (supportive, compassionate, enlightened) helps build healthier, more harmonious relationships at all levels

Time Balance Scale

This scale helps you see where your focus is—whether on the past, present, or future. Knowing this can help you use your time better and keep your energy focused on what matters most.

104°F-102°F

Focus Level	Description		Time Balance	Main Focus
Stuck in Past/ Future	104°F	Focused on past regrets	Past (50%) + Future (30%) + Present (20%)	Mostly focused on regrets or worries about the future
	103°F	Worried about the future		
	102°F	Trapped in thoughts of the past or future		

101°F-100°F

Focus Level	Description		Time Balance	Main Focus
Growing	101°F	Breaking old patterns	Past (25%) + Future (30%) + Present (45%)	Balancing learning, planning, and growth
	100.5°F	Exploring new ideas		
	100°F	Embracing change		

99°F-98°F

Focus Level	Description		Time Balance	Main Focus
Balanced	99°F	Mindful action	Past (10%) + Future (15%) + Present (75%)	Focused on present with minimal distractions
	98.6°F	Clear purpose		
	98°F	Inner peace		

Why Staying Present Matters

The present moment is where we make choices and take action. By focusing on the present, we set the stage for our future and avoid getting stuck in regrets or worries. Staying present helps us make each moment count and build a life of mindful, purpose-driven actions.

Summary of Focus Levels

1. 104°F - 102°F (Stuck in Past/Future)
Mostly focused on past regrets or future worries.
Impact: High stress, less focus on current tasks.

2. 101°F - 100°F (Growing)
Reflecting on the past and planning the future while growing in
the present.
Impact: Supports personal growth and helps with daily goals.

3. 99°F - 98°F (Balanced)
Balanced focus on past, future, and present, mostly staying in the present.
Impact: Better clarity, lower stress, and effective productivity.

Here's a general guide to how the body may feel at different temperatures:

- 98°F: Normal body temperature, feeling relaxed and comfortable.

- 99°F: Slightly warm, but still within the normal range.

- 100°F: Mild fever, may feel slightly warm, sweaty, or tired.

- 101°F: Fever is more noticeable, may feel hot, sweaty, or experience mild headaches.

- 102°F: Moderate fever, may feel weak, tired, or experience more severe headaches.

- 103°F: Fever is more intense, may feel dizzy, disoriented, or experience muscle aches.

- 104°F: High fever, may feel extremely weak, tired, or experience severe headaches, confusion, or disorientation.

Tips to Release Limiting Beliefs:

Recognizing and challenging limiting beliefs is essential for personal growth and improvement. These beliefs can hold us back from achieving our full potential, causing unnecessary stress, anxiety, and self-doubt. In this guide, we will explore common limiting beliefs, categorized by past, present, and future.

Past-Based Limiting Beliefs

1. Overgeneralization: Believing that one negative experience represents a universal truth.

2. Holding Regrets: Holding onto past regrets, which can lead to feelings of guilt and "what ifs."

3. Past Trauma: Believing that past traumas define one's current and future potential.

4. Ancestral Patterns: Limiting beliefs inherited from ancestors, perpetuating patterns of thought and behavior.

Present-Based Limiting Beliefs

1. Fixed Mindset: Believing that abilities and intelligence are fixed, rather than developable.

2. Negative Self-Talk: Criticizing oneself, which can lead to low self-esteem and confidence.

3. Perfectionism: Believing that mistakes are unacceptable, which can lead to anxiety and paralysis.

4. Scarcity Mindset: Believing that resources are limited, which can lead to competition and hoarding.

5. Societal Expectations: Believing that one must conform to societal norms, rather than forging one's own path.

6. Classism: Believing that one's socioeconomic status determines opportunities or abilities.

7. **Superstition Beliefs:** Believing in superstitions, suchas:

> 1. Not crossing the road after a cat has crossed.

> 2. Not cutting nails on certain days.

Future-Based Limiting Beliefs

1. **Fear-Based Beliefs:** Fearing failure, rejection, or success, which can hold individuals back from taking risks.

2. **Fatalism:** Believing that one's life is predetermined, and that personal choices have no impact.

3. **Lack of Purpose:** Believing that life has no inherent meaning or purpose.

4. **Lack of Faith:** Believing that one is alone, and that there is no higher power or guidance.

Emotional Limiting Beliefs

1. **Holding Anger:** Holding onto anger and resentment towards oneself or others.

2. **Jealousy:** Believing that someone else's success or happiness diminishes one's own.

3. **Believing** Others are Responsible for One's Happiness: Believing that someone else's presence or absence determines one's happiness or success.

Conclusion

Recognizing and challenging limiting beliefs is a powerful step towards personal growth and improvement. By understanding and overcoming these beliefs, individuals can break free from constraints and achieve their full potential. Remember, it's never too late to change your mindset and unlock a brighter future.

The Mental Fever Analogy

Just as emotional turmoil can ravage our mental well-being, overly thinking about the past or future can similarly 'infect' our minds. When we excessively dwell on past regrets or worry about future uncertainties, our minds become a breeding ground for wasteful thoughts. These unnecessary mental exertions exhaust our mental energy, much like a prolonged fever depletes our physical vitality. Often, this mental fever is fueled by the toxic impact of limiting beliefs. When we're held hostage by negative self-talk, fear, or doubt, our minds can become trapped in a vicious cycle of anxious thinking. By recognizing and challenging these limiting beliefs, we can break free from the mental fever that's holding us back and unlock a more peaceful, productive, and fulfilling life.

Break Free

> **"**
>
> *Limiting beliefs are like shadows of mere illusion and not the walls : they disappear when exposed to the light of awareness and the power of self-reflection.*
>
> **"**

-Rajeev Kharyal

Thought Focus Scale

Assess your concentration and mental clarity, and develop strategies to enhance your productivity and goal-oriented mindset.

Let's determine your level of focus using the focus scale. How many of your daily thoughts are directed toward your goals and priorities?

Find out where you stand on the 1-7 focus level scale.

	Level 1	Level 2	Level 3	Level 4	Level 5	Level 6	Level 7
Power of level	6/60	6/36	6/24	6/18	6/12	6/9	6/6
Thoughts Per Day	60000	36000	24000	18000	12000	9000	6000

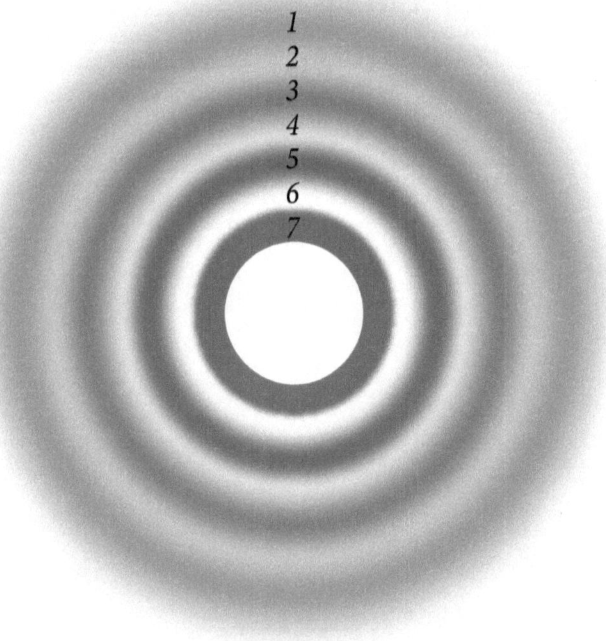

Focus Scale Categories: Levels of Clarity and Purpose

This scale shows different levels of focus, from crystal-clear goals to drifting without direction, using relatable titles and a Gold Purity level as a symbol of clarity.

Vision Level	Focus Category	Title	Description	Gold Purity
6/6 Vision	Crystal Clear	The Clarity Keeper	Has perfect clarity about goals and purpose, seeing challenges and opportunities clearly.	24K
6/9 Vision	Focused Clarity	The Goal Getter	Knows the direction well but may need small adjustments to stay fully on track.	23K
6/12 Vision	Blurred Horizons	The Pathfinder	Purpose feels a bit unclear; needs reflection to find the right direction.	22K
6/18 Vision	Faded Focus	The Seeker	Feels somewhat lost and needs guidance or self-awareness to find clarity again.	20K
6/24 Vision	Distracted Vision	The Navigator	Struggles to stay focused without help; needs clear guidance to refocus on goals.	18K
6/36 Vision	Lost Sight	The Drifter	Lacks clear goals and drifts; may need a major change or support to regain direction.	16K
6/60 Vision	Blind Spots	The Dreamer	Has big dreams but lacks the focus to reach them; needs transformation to turn dreams into action.	14K

Key Takeaway

This scale helps readers identify their current level of focus and understand what steps they can take to gain greater clarity and purpose. The gold purity scale symbolizes how refined and clear each level of focus is

The 3A Framework: Accelerating Excellence Through Self-Reflection

Transform Your Journey from Mindset 84 to 13 to 3 with Awareness, Acceptance, and Action

Once self-assessments through various diagnostic tools are completed, embark on the 3A journey:

A1: Awareness - Understand Your Current Landscape Receive insightful feedback from assessment scales, Recognize strengths, weaknesses, opportunities, and threats, Acknowledge areas for improvement and growth

A2: Acceptance - Embrace Your Reality Honestly confront your current situation, Let go of denial, resistance, or negativity, Cultivate self-compassion and openness to change

A3: Action - Drive Excellence with SMART Goals Set Specific, Measurable, Achievable, Relevant, and Time-bound objectives, Develop a tailored plan to bridge gaps and leverage strengths, Embed accountability and tracking mechanisms for sustained progress

> *Key Takeaways:*
>
> *Introspection ignites the 3A framework, Awareness, Acceptance, and Action synergize for breakthroughs, Continuous assessment and adjustment propel your excellence journey.*

Embracing Destiny's Role in Your Journey to Excellence

As I strive to transition from Mindset 84 to 13 to 3, I often wonder: Is destiny limiting my progress? It's crucial to understand destiny's influence on our lives.

According to ancient wisdom: Destiny is the culmination of past karma, manifesting as life's situations, people, and experiences. Yet, our responses to these circumstances are shaped by our present choices, exercising free will.

In essence:

- Past karma shapes current destiny (situations, people, places)

- Present responses forge new karma (choices, actions)

- Future destiny unfolds based on current karma

Recognizethat destiny presents opportunities, but your responses determine the outcome. Harness this understanding to:

Embrace challenges as growth catalysts, Exercise mindful choices, Shape your future destiny with intentional actions

Your journey to excellence is not predetermined; it's a dynamic interplay between destiny and self-directed karma."

12 Dimensions of Human Excellence Snapshot

For real-life applications and future reference, revisit these essential dimensions:

1. Mindset Mastery: 84% Doers, 13% Thinkers, 3% Masterminds
2. Intelligence Quotients: SQ (Spiritual), EQ (Emotional), IQ (Intellectual)
3. Energetic Balance: Sun (Creativity), Moon (Intuition), Earth (Stability)
4. Character Carats: Authenticity, Empathy, Resilience, Integrity
5. Achievement Levels: Gold (Excellence), Silver (Growth), Bronze (Foundation)
6. Intent Power: Focus, Clarity, Purpose
7. Solution Mindset: Heating Up for Innovative Solutions
8. Non-Verbal Intelligence: Effective Communication, Active Listening
9. Relationship Dynamics: 36 Gunas (Traits) for Harmonious Connections
10. Focus and Productivity: From Voltage to Focus
11. Timeless Awareness: Past, Future, Present Mindfulness
12. Operating Voltage: Optimize Your Energy Levels

Refer to this snapshot to:

- Refresh your understanding of the 12 Dimensions
- Apply principles to real-life situations
- Reflect on your progress and growth

> *Embedding these dimensions into your daily life will propel you toward human excellence.*

12 Dimensions of Human Excellence

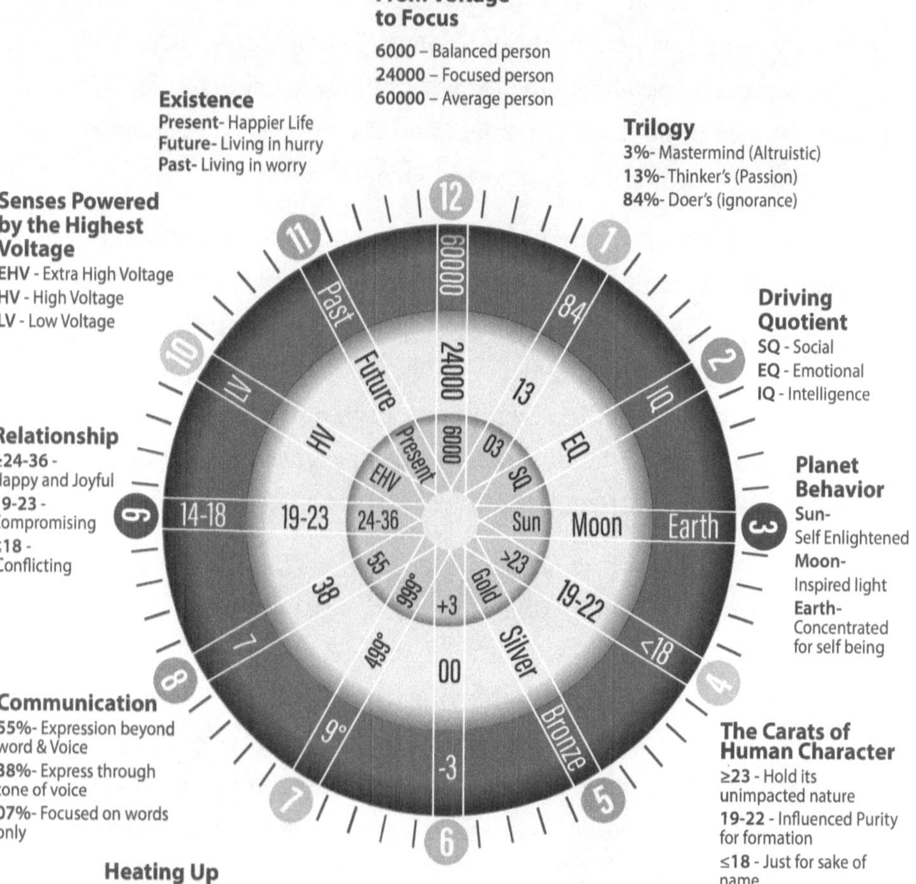

From Voltage to Focus

6000 – Balanced person
24000 – Focused person
60000 – Average person

Trilogy

3%- Mastermind (Altruistic)
13%- Thinker's (Passion)
84%- Doer's (ignorance)

Existence

Present- Happier Life
Future- Living in hurry
Past- Living in worry

Senses Powered by the Highest Voltage

EHV - Extra High Voltage
HV - High Voltage
LV - Low Voltage

Driving Quotient

SQ - Social
EQ - Emotional
IQ - Intelligence

Relationship

≥24-36 - Happy and Joyful
19-23 - Compromising
≤18 - Conflicting

Planet Behavior

Sun- Self Enlightened
Moon- Inspired light
Earth- Concentrated for self being

Communication

55%- Expression beyond word & Voice
38%- Express through tone of voice
07%- Focused on words only

The Carats of Human Character

≥23 - Hold its unimpacted nature
19-22 - Influenced Purity for formation
≤18 - Just for sake of name

Heating Up for Solutions

999° - Casting in desired shape (only focused toward's their action)
499° - Right Time Right Action (timely response)
9° - Striking Cold iron (immediate response)

The Power of Intent

+3 | Carry positive attributes
0 | Swings between the two
-3 | Carry negative attributes

Metal Value

Gold - Mkt cost is 100 times to Silver
Silver - Mkt cost is 100 times to bronze
Bronze - Consider cost 1

Dedication and Gratitude

As I complete this book, I am overwhelmed with a deep sense of gratitude. First and foremost, I dedicate this work to my family—Suruchi, Rajeev (myself), Meenakshi, and Smriti, affectionately referred as **SRAMS** in short form. Their unwavering love, support, and honest feedback have been the pillars that helped bring the ideas within these pages to life. It is my sincere hope that my readers find the same kind of support and encouragement in their own journeys.

I am profoundly thankful to my colleagues and friends—S/Sh Gian Chand and Rohit Sharma who have played an role in shaping the thoughts and ideas shared here, grounded in my personal experiences.I extend my heartfelt thanks to all those who contributed in their own unique ways and to everyone who provided feedback as this book took shape; your faith in me has been a source of strength that I will forever cherish.

Finally, my sincere gratitude goes to PREM NGO, where my journey of conducting Life Skills sessions began nearly a decade ago. Faced with the challenge of explaining these concepts to young students, starting from class VII, I discovered the transformative power of analogies in simplifying complex ideas. This experience became the cornerstone of my approach, allowing me to share life's essential lessons in ways that resonate deeply and meaningfully.

And from the core of my heart, I extend a profound gratitude that words cannot capture to my Guru, who has illuminated my path. While the mistakes are my own, the journey ahead continues, with the lessons I have yet to fully embrace.

About The Author

Rajeev Kharyal

With over 35 years of pioneering experience in the power distribution industry, Rajeev Kharyal has established himself as a visionary leader. As Chief Commercial Officer at Tata Power Central Odisha Distribution Limited, he spearheaded initiatives that transformed customer experience, advanced smart metering, and optimized business operations. His groundbreaking work at Tata Power DDL contributed significantly to the company's growth by embedding excellence through structured frameworks like TBEM and TQM. His efforts also elevated India's Ease of Doing Business ranking in electricity, aligning with global standards. He led Tata Power DDL's "Urja Arpan" initiative, a pioneering program focused on climate action and sustainability. He is known for his exceptional communication skills, which include effective presentations, innovative problem-solving, first-principle thinking, and a creative mindset. Beyond his corporate leadership, Rajeev Kharyal has advised central and state ministries on power sector reforms, sustainability policies, and customer service enhancements. A techno-commercial expert, he holds a B.Tech in Electrical Engineering from NIT Warangal and is an alumnus of IIM Bangalore. As a certified Grow More corporate life coach, Rajeev Kharyal is deeply committed to empowering young professionals to achieve personal and career success. With a passion for impactful growth, he inspires and mentors the next generation of leaders. His favorite quotes, which inspire his team, are: "Winners do not do different things, they do things differently" from Shiv Khera's book "You Can Win", and his own guiding principle, "Intent behind Doing an Act Drives the Outcome."

Blurb

Unlock the Hidden Code to Holistic Success

Imagine living a life where purpose, fulfillment, and success align. This transformative guide reveals the secret patterns and practical tools to:

- Assess yourself across IQ, EQ, and SQ
- Harness the 3A framework: Awareness, Acceptance, and Action
- Embark on the 3E journey: Experience, Express, and Evolve

By applying these principles with easy understanding through analogies , you'll develop essential skills for thriving in the AI era, including First-Principle Thinking, Effective Communication, and Value-Driven Agility.

Join the 3% who have cracked the code to holistic success. Transform your mindset from Fixed to Growth to Evolved, and unlock your full potential. Start your journey today!

Let this guide be your companion in becoming the best version of yourself and inspiring greatness in those around you.